GYPSY-ENGLISH
ENGLISH-GYPSY
CONCISE DICTIONARY

D1571539

GYPSY-ENGLISH
ENGLISH-GYPSY
CONCISE DICTIONARY

ATANAS SLAVOV

HIPPOCRENE BOOKS, INC.
New York

With gratitude to the International Center for Minority Studies and International Relations for its support.

ISBN 0-7818-0775-1

For information, address:
HIPPOCRENE BOOKS, INC.
171 Madison Avenue
New York, NY 10016

Printed in the United States of America.

CONTENTS

INTRODUCTION

Bulgarian Gypsies

According to *The Webster Dictionary*, "Gypsies are Caucasoid people coming originally from India to Europe in the 14TH or 15TH century."

The territory of present day Bulgaria, Turkey and Greece was the first place in Europe to be reached by the Gypsies some three centuries earlier. During the Byzantine occupation of Bulgaria from 1019 to 1185, Armenian troops were brought in to quell Bulgarian armed unrest. Linguists have traced elements in the language of Bulgarian Gypsies which show that the immediate descendants of those Armenians had lived side by side with Gypsies who already had established themselves here from their homeland in India. Two hundred years later the Bulgarian king Shishman (1371–1393) gave (by decree) a couple of villages to the Rila monastery in which Gypsies already lived a settled life.

This makes the Bulgarian Gypsy dialects of particular interest to anyone who is curious about Gypsies and the Romany language.

The Language and its Dialects

The Gypsy language is spoken by a good half a million people in Bulgaria and probably close to 5 million throughout Europe. The vocabulary of present day Romany, like other Balkan languages, is a symbiosis of original Romany words and aspects of Turkish, Bulgarian and Greek.

Different authors claim the existence of more than a dozen Gypsy dialects in Bulgaria. Bulgarian Gypsies speaking one dialect though are easily understood by Gypsies speaking other dialects as well as by Gypsies from all over the world.

This dictionary reflects the vocabulary of two Bulgarian Gypsy dialects: the Sofia Erli dialect and the dialect of the Christian Gypsies of Sliven.

The Sofia Erli dialect is a natural choice for a number of reasons. First of all, the Erli dialect is widespread throughout Europe which hopefully will make this dictionary workable in many countries. Aside of that the capital of Bulgaria Sofia has the largest Gypsy population in that country. This makes their native Erli dialect better protected and preserved from outside influences in comparison to the dialects of other Gypsy groups around the Balkans. Finally, the Erli dialect is best studied by Bulgarian linguists and Romany scholars throughout the world.

The Sliven Christian Gypsies are the oldest single-dialect *and* settled Gypsy city population in present day Bulgaria. Approximately 160 years ago, a reform related to the modernization of the Ottoman Empire took place which called for the massive textile production of the uniforms for the newly established regular Turkish army. A state textile factory was subsequently built in Sliven. Because the new laws prohibited non-Moslem workers from participating in state production, Moslem Gypsies were dragged forceably into town from all over and made work in the factory as well as in other military projects in Sliven. Relatively well paid, housed and protected by the time Bulgaria became independent, they had become what Gypsies call a "baro" tribe, or "Big Ones," i.e. well established Gypsies. After the First World War, the Sliven Gypsies were Christianized and nourished numerous scholars, lawyers, musicians, etc. of national significance. In addition, Sliven boasts the most dense Gypsy city population in Bulgaria speaking a single permanently established dialect. Statistics show that they form up to 8% of the city's population of approximately 130 000, representing 11,000 citizens who have been living there for more than 160 years. Other clusters of dense Gypsy communities unfortunately speak a hodge-podge of Gypsy dialects which are very unstable and thus cannot serve our purposes.

Entries of interest from other Gypsy dialects have been included sporadically in this work for reasons of comparison mainly from the Balkans (Serbian, Romanian, Turkish, Greek) and the Near East (Armenian, Persian).

We have not marked consistently throughout the dictionary the dialect which every word belongs to. However, for important cases, we indicate the dialect by using (e) for "Erli" words, (s) for Sliven dialect words, (vlh) for Romanian, (srb) for Serbian, (grk) for Greek, (trk) for Turkish, (arm) for Armenian, and (prs) for Persian.

Sources

Aside from the well known academic works this dictionary has been compiled from several unwritten sources, the first one being the author's collection of Sofia street jargons and student slang from the 1940s which contains more than 1,000 entries of Gypsy language origin.

During 1998, six Sliven Christian Gypsies, and one Sofia Erli Gypsy were interviewed on the vocabulary of the dictionary. The oldest was a 91 year old former textile worker and the youngest a 22-year old university student. The research was supported by the Bulgarian International Center for Minority Studies and International Relations.

ALPHABET AND PHONETICS

Alphabet

For the time being there is no common Gypsy alphabet not only around the world but even for the Bulgarian Gypsy dialects in spite of the occasional Romany language publications in that country.

The following letters and letter combinations are used for the Gypsy words in this dictionary:

a, b, ch, csh, d, e, f, g, h, i, j, k, kh, l, lr, m, n, o, oo, p, ph, r, s, sh, t, th, ts, u, v, w, y, z, zh

We do not give a phonetic transcription for the Gypsy worlds in this dictionary since the alphabet we are using is a phonetic alphabet by itself.

Phonetics

The following letters and letter combinations are used for the phonemes in the Gypsy language that have no obvious corresponding letters in the English alphabet:

a -	as in g**o**t
ch -	as in **ch**at
csh -	no corresponding sound exists in English. It is a "ch" sound (like in **ch**at) aspirated with the fricative "sh" (like in ea**ch sh**oe)
e -	as in **e**nd
g -	as in **g**ot
j -	as in **j**oy
k -	as in **c**at
kh -	aspirated "k" (approximately as in in**k-h**orn)
lr -	no corresponding sound exists in English. The closest description of it would be to prepare ones mouth for the pronunciation of "l" and then try to pronounce "r" with the same position of the tongue in the mouth.
o -	as in s**o**mber, or b**a**ll
oo -	as in b**oo**t
ph -	aspirated "p" (like in u**ph**ill)
sh -	as in **sh**ow
th -	aspirated "t" (approximately as in a**t-h**and or ho**t-h**eels)
ts -	as in **Ts**ar, or Puli**tz**er
u -	as in b**u**rn, or l**o**ve, or f**i**rst
w -	as in co**w**, or **w**ater
zh -	as in trea**s**ure

à, è, ì, ò, ù, òo - stressed vowels

` - A stress sign on a vowel, denoting the word
   stress

As mentioned above, we do not give a phonetic transcription for the Gypsy worlds in this dictionary since the alphabet we are using is a
phonetic alphabet by itself. The Romany in this
work is an orthographic language in which each
sound is represented by its own letter or letter
combination, which is pronounced consistently
the same way. *In short, words are pronounced
exactly as they appear.*

Word stress does not play a significant role in
the Gypsy language. It is presented in this work
the way words were pronounced by the Gypsies
we interviewed. If the interviewees or the written
sources we used show differences in applying
stresses in certain words, we do not show them.

ABBREVIATIONS

adj.	adjective
adv.	adverb
(arm)	Armenian
art.	article
(bot)	botanical
conj.	conjunction
(e)	the dialect of the Erli Gypsies from Sofia
f.	feminine
(grk)	Greek
imp.	imperative
intj.	interjection
int.	interrogative
lit.	literary
m.	masculine
n.	noun
(prs)	Persian
pl.	plural
p.n.	proper name
pron.	pronoun
prep.	preposition
refl.	reflective
(s)	the dialect of the Sliven Christian Gypsies
(srb)	Serbian
(sl)	slang
(trk)	Turkish
v.	verb

(vlh)	Romanian
voc.	vocative
vulg.	vulgar

NUMERALS

ekh	one
dooy	two
trin	three
shtar	four
panch	five
shov	six
eftà	seven
ohtò	eight
eynà	nine
desh	ten
deshooèk	eleven
dooshoodòoy	twelve
deshootrìn	thirteen
deshooshtàr	fourteen
deshoopànch	fifteen
deshooshòv	sixteen
desheftà	seventeen
deshohtò	eighteen
desheynà	nineteen
bish, besh	twenty
triyànda	thirty
sarànda	forty
peìnda	fifty
shovàrdesh	sixty
eftavàrdesh	seventy

ohtovàrdesh	eighty
eynavàrdesh	ninety
shel	hundred
dòoyshel	two hundred
trìnshel	three hundred
shtàrshel	four hundred
pànchshel	five hundred
shòvshel	six hundred
eftàshel	seven hundred
ohtòshel	eight hundred
eynàshel	nine hundred
mìlya	thousand
desh milyà	two thousand
triyànda milyà	three thousand
sarànda milya	four thousand
peìnda milyà	five thousand
etc.	

Names of some dice faces in backgammon

1+1	hep ekh	4+1	jar o ekv
2+2	dooy barò [i.e. "big two"]	5+1	penj o ekh
3+3	dooy se	5+2	penj o dooy
4+4	dyort jar	5+3	penj o trin
5+5	dooy besh	6+5	shesh besh
6+6	dooy shesh	6+1	shesh o ekh

GYPSY-ENGLISH DICTIONARY

A

abè (sl) n. bread
abèjiya (sl) n. baker
aboorkà adv. that much
absìn n. steel
achàv v. leave, stay
achòo adj. pretty
achookà (e) so
acsh! (e) imp. stop!
acshàv (e) v. stop
acshiye dale (s) [pejorative term for a lowlife
      social group]
acshòv devlèsa! goodbye!
adalkèske that is why
adavkà pron. this
adavkhà pron. this
adekhì (e) that much
adèti n. custom
adètsi n. custom
adì prep. in, into [gelo andi pani "went into the
      water"]
aeroplànoos n. airplane
aglàl adv. in front
agor n. end

agorinò adj. the last one
agoroonò adj. last
agorù adv. at the end
ahayas n. business deal
ahayàva (s) v. understand
ahaylè adj. understood
ahmàki n. fool
ahmàtsi manoosh foolish man
ahtè adv. here
ahùri n. stables
ajaràv v. expect
akanà adv. now
akanà n. name
akàndav (e) v. serve, help
akanootnò adj. present, contemporary
akavkà pron. m., this
akaykà pron. f., this
akè adv. here
akhor n. walnut
akhyàr! imp. yell! call!
akhyaràv v. call
akooròo (s) n. ceramic pitcher
akòosh! imp. curse!
akooshàv (e) v. curse
akooshàva (s) v. curse
akooshìba (e) n. curse
akooshibè (s) n. curse
àla n. aunt

alàv n. name [sar si to alav? "what is your name?"]

alàv n. word

alrò (s) egg

amà prep. but

amàl (prs) n. friend

amalipè n. friendship

amarò (e) pron. our

amaròo (s) pron. our

ambaròo (s) pron. ours

ambròl n. pear

ambrolìn n. pear tree

amè (e) pron. we

amìn (s) pron. we, us

amnaryòo n. flint and steel

amunì n. anvil

an! imp. give! ["mande an" give it to me]

an ahtè! imp. bring here!

Anatolàte p.n. Asia Minor

Anatoliyà p.n., Asia Minor

anàv v. bring

andàr prep, from

andarò prep. from

andèr adj. soft [as in "the soft inside part of the bread"]

andìnav v. mention

andiyavìn n. f. morning

andò adv. before

andràl adv. from the inside
andrè adv. inside
andronibe n. bowels, guts, intestines
androonò adj. inside
angàl adj. front, in front
angàr n. coal
àngelas n. angel
angloonò adj. first
angoosh n. toe
angooshtò (e) n. finger
angooshtòo (s) n. finger
angroostsì (s) n. ring
an gùy dyàva v. embrace
angyàr! imp. bring
angyarèlpes n. showing ones tongue
anìtsi (e) n. rice
anolàv (e) v. tin-plate
ànolima (e) n. tin-plating
anta! imp. bring!
antava v. bring
àpakyaba (e) n. faith, belief
apakyàv (e) v. believe
aphai n. apple
aprasaba n. criticism
aprasàv v. ridicule, criticize
aptsin (s) n. steel
arabajìdes n. cart driver
arabajìs n. cart driver

arakhav v. find [arakhav o drom "find the road"]
arakhlò adj. found
arakhlò adj. saved
aràva (e) v. ruin, spoil,
aravdò adj. spoiled
arazhyava v. lose weight
arazyava v. lose weight
archich (arm.) n. tin
arlì n. deal
Arliye n. [the name of the Sofia Moslem Gypsy tribe]
armagànos n. gift
armanyà n. pledge
armi n. sauercraut
arò (e) (s) n. flour
aròo (s) n. flour
àsaba n. laughter
asanòo mànoosh adj. smiling man, all smiles
asàv (e) v. laugh
asàva (s) v. smile
asavkà (e) such
ashamò (e) n. wrestler
ashàr! imp. wrestle!
asharàv (e) n. wrestle
asharàv v. boast
asharàva (s) n. wrestle
asharàva v. praise
ashardinav v. morning sickness (pregnancy)

àshariba (e) wrestling match, fight
asharibè n. wrestling
ashàshibe (e) n. puke
ashchì v. can [ashchi keràv adavkà "I can do this"]
ashtà! imp. hand over!
ashtipè n. possibility
asìya n. club
askèri n. soldier
aslàni n. lion
aslùy (s) n. lion
àsoos (s) n. tear
astar! imp. begin!
astaràv v. get, start
astaràv v. touch, hold
astaràva (s) v. catch
àsva (e) n. tear
asvày n. water mill
asvayèngoro n. miller
asvìn n. tear
asyàv n. m. mill
asyavjìs n. m. miller
athartoonò adj. local
athavdàv v. run, flow
athè adv. here
atmazhas (s) n. falcon
auràri n. goldpanner, the name of the "goldpanners" Gypsy tribe

avàv v. come
avàva v. arrive
avdiès adv. today
avdisootnò adj. today's
avèr (sl) n. friend, from the same gang
avèr adj. another, foreign
avgìn n. honey
avginyatar adj. honey
avgò adj. first
avìn n. dawn, morning [Bahtalì ti avin! "Good morning!"]
avlìn n. yard, barn, field
avrehtè adv. another place
avrès adj. pron. another
avrì adv. outside
avroonò adj. outside
aynàs n. mirror
àyos n. baptism, christening
ayrùi n. yoghurt soft drink
azdimè adj. absent-minded [mi gozì nanùy thanèsti "my brain is not in its place"]
azdinav v. joke, tease
azdrahìli (e) n. teaser
azmàtsi n. swamp

B
babà (rare) n. father
bàberka n. leftover fruit after fruit-gathering

badàvaman v. rise
bahchà n. vegetable garden
bahchovanjìs n. gardener, vegetable
    grower
baht (srb) n. happiness
bahtàli (srb) n. white magic
bahtalò (e) adj. happy [bahtalo to alav "happy
    name-day"]
bakh (s) n. happiness, luck
bakhalò n. hunger
bakhalòosi (s) n. hunger
bakranò adj. sheep
bakrì n. sheep, ewe
bakrò n. lamb
bakròo (s) n. ram
bakshìshi n. tip
bal (e) n. hair, lock, bird plume
bala (s) n. hair
balalò adj. hairy
balamò (sl) n. fool
balamò n. Greek
balanì n. trough
balanì n. tub, washtub
balen-charàv v. herd swine
balì n. sow
balichkanò adj. pig, swine
balichkanò adj. pork
balichò n. piglet

balicshnì (e) n. f. sow
Balkàn p.n. Balkans
balkòy n. balcony
balò n. m. pig, swine
balr n. stone
balr (s) n. stone
balùy n. tub
balvàl n. wind
balval (s) n. storm
bandrooki n. yoke
bandzyàva v. bend
bang n. drum
bangaryàv v. bend
bangè adj. bent
bangèste adj. crooked
bangipè n. injustice
bangò adj. crooked, bent
bangò adj. lame
bangòo mànoosh (s) n. hunchback, cripple
bangyà adj. crooked
bangyaràv v. bend
bangyaràv v. make a turn
bangyardò adj. bent
bànka n. bank
bar n. fence, stone
barà (s) n. pl. rocks, stones
bàra n. limit, border
barèma adv. at least

bàrema adv. at least (barema manoosh te avel
      "if he at least was a [real] man")
barèstar adj. out of stone
Barì dis (rare) p. n. Sofia
barikanò adj. proud
barìpe n. big thing, great thing
barkanò n. mutton, lamb meat
bar morìskoo (s) n. gravestone
barò (e) adj. big
barò màsek n. January
baròo (s) adj. big
baròo angooshtoo n. thumb
baròo chòokoos (s) n. mallet
baroonì adj. stone [barooni proot "stone bridge"]
baròotsi n. gunpowder
barvalipè n. wealth
barvalò (e) adj. wealthy, rich
barvalòo (s) adj. wealthy, rich
barvaypì n. riches
barvilivàva v. become rich
baryovà v. grow
bas (s) n. wager [basista astrarsatoot "to make a
      bet." Lit.: to "lay" a gamble]
basamàtsya n. pl. staircase steps
bashàla (sl) v. play music
bashalàv (e) v. play music
bashalàv (s) v. bark, crow, make sounds
bashalàva (s) v. play music

bashaldòo (s) n. musician
bashalipè n. music
bashalnò n. musician
bashàv (e) v. bark, crow, make sounds
bàshilba n. music
bashnò (e) n. rooster
bashnòo (s) n. rooster
bastòoy (s) n. cane, walking stick
bastòy (e) n. cane
batalo (srb) adj. happy
batonàva v. sink
bay n. sleeve
bayàv (s) n. wedding
baychòo (s) n. f. pig
baycshonòo adj. pork
baynàv v. charm, cast a spell
bayràtsi (s) n. flag
bejìti adj. missing
belàs n. nuisance, mischief, trouble
belyàke (e) adv. tonight
belyàte adv. evening time
bèna (s) v. hatch, bear
beng n. devil
bengalò n. epileptic
bengikanè adj. devil's
bengikanò adj. devilish
bengipè n. trick
berànda n. support at the center of the tent

berolì (e) n. bee
beroolì (s) n. bee
berorì n. bee
bersh n. year
bertimè adj. sprained
bertinàv v. sprain
besh n. forest
besh n. twenty
besh! imp. sit!
beshàv v. stay, sit
beshipè n. anniversary
beshlyardò adj. cut
beshlyoràv v. stick, thrust
beshnyà n. squatting
beshtòo (s) adj. seated
bèteltsa n. hoe, pick
bèti adj. uncomfortable, uneasy, awkward [sosi
      mange "how uneasy I am!"]
bezè n. sin
bezèti n. dream, wish
bi (e) without
bi-akhàkero adj. blind
bi-balèngero adj. bald
bì-balìngoo adj. bald
bi-chalò (e) adj. unsatisfiable, insatiable
bi-chavèngero adj. childless
bi-dandèngoro n. toothless
bi-godiàtero adj. mindless, irresponsible

bi-kokalàngero adj. boneless
bi-lachò adj. bad
bi-lajalò adj. shameless
bi-milò adj. immortal
bi-parèngoro adj. penniless
bi-romnyàkoro adj. bachelor
biabàh n. bad luck
biamal (e) n. enemy
bianàv v. bear
bibahtali (srb) n. black magic
bibe-koro n. cousin
bibì n. aunt
bibì n. grandmother
bibì! voc. You grandmother!
bìbitsa n. turkey
Bibiyaka (srb) p.n. Black Sara [May Day goddess]
bichalàv (e) v. send, put aside, arrange
bichalàva (s) v. send
bìchos n. whip
bigogipè n. recklessness, foolhardedness
bijardò adj. unexpected
bikenàva (e) v. sell
bikendò adj. sold
bìkeniba (e) n. sale
bikìnava (s) v. sell
bìkoos (s) n. bull
bìkos (e) n. bull

bikyanàv v. sell
bikyanibè n. sale
bilaiba n. melt
bilastsimi (s) adj. tasteless
bilàv v. melt
bilavdò adj. melted
bimarìbe n. peace
bìra n. beer
birdèn adv. suddenly, soon
bish n. twenty
bish milyà n. twenty thousand
bishtò adj. twentieth
bisteràv (e) v. forget
bisterdò adj. forgotten
bistràva (s) v. forget
boàzi n. gorge
bòboos n. beans
bof n. stove, furness
boholyàchi n. monster
bòhos n. bull
boimlis v. baptize
bok n. hunger
bokalyàv v. become hungry
boldò n. best man, godfather
boldò v. christen
boldò v. dip in water
bonèla (s) n. fork
boohaloos (s) n. owl

boohlipè (e) n. width
boohlò (e) adj. wide
boohlyaràv v. spread, stretch
boohlyardò adj. widened, stretched
boohlyaribè n. bedspread
boojando (e) n. understanding
boojandò n. knowledgeable
book n. beech tree
bòoka n. bite
bookagìes n. handcuffs, chains
bookli n. pl. curls
bookò n. innards, liver
bookyàrnegeri (e) adj. worker's
bookyarnò n. worker
bool n. ass, behind, genitals [del man boole mo
      rom "my husband is tupping me"]
boolòoti n. cloud
boolyàkoro n. thigh
boolyàkoro marò (sl) n. bread received after a
      lot of begging [lit.: a lot of banging of the
      beggar's bag against the buttocks]
boonàri n. well
boonzharàv v. pin up
boonzharàv v. turn up (boonzharav me baya
      "turn up my sleeves"]
boorgìya n. drill
boorgoodjìdes n. pl. Gypsy ironsmiths
boorgoodjìs n. ironsmith, blacksmith

---

boorgòon n. drill
boornèk n. handfull, palm
bòoryanoos (s) n. weed
boot adv. much, more, a lot
bootì n. work
booti keràv v. work
bootlàchoo (s) adj. nice, tasty
bootòoshi (s) n. boots
bootsyarnoo (s) n. workoholic
boozì (s) n. goat
boozi ekomas n. goat meat
booznì (e) n. goat
boozò n. billy goat
borchlìs n. debtor
borì n. bride
borì n. daughter-in-law
bòroos n. pine
bov (arm) n. oven, stove
boyà n. color paint
boza n. Balkan soft drink
Bozhìk n. Christmas
bràdva n. ax
bratovchèdka n. f. cousin
bratovchèdoos (s) n. m. cousin
brekh n. bosom
bresh n. year
brezà n. birch tree
bridvà adj. picked
brishìm (s) n. rain

brishìm del v. rain v.
brishimdalò adj. rainy
brishìnt (s) n. rain
brivàv (e) v. card (wool)
brivàva (s) v. card (wool)
brivdò (e) adj. plucked
brùchka (s) n. wrinkle n.
brusnàchi (s) n. razor n.
bryàgoos n. river-bank
bùlnoozyava v. talk in one's sleep
buychòo (s) n. pig
buzni (pers) n. goat
byav n. wedding

Ch
chachès (e) n. truth
chachestè adj. really
chachì rig (srb) n. right-hand side
chachipe (srb) n. tradition [romano chachipe
    "Gypsy tradition"]
chachoonò adj. real
chachoonò adj. righteous
chadàv v. vomit
chadimè adj. dingy
chadinàv v. smoke
chadùri n. umbrella
chak as far as
chakhùy (s) n. gravel

chakmàk n. flint and iron
chakmàkoos (s) n. flint and iron
chakrùk n. spinning wheel
chakùi n. gravel
chakùl n. gravel, rubble
chakuzhìs n. gravel worker
chalà! imp. blow!
chàlaiba (e) n. strike
chalàstra (sl) v. drink [from: "strike one." See "chalav"]
chalàv! imp. hit!
chalàv v. hit
chalàva v. blow, bloat
chalavàv v. hit, strike the aim
chalavdò adj. hit, stricken, wounded
chalaybè n. strike
chàlga n. Gypsy music
chalgajìs n. musician
chàliba n. strike
chalkìya n. fool
chalkìya n. guitar
chalò adj. sated, satisfied
chalyàr! imp. satisfy!
chalyardò adj. full, satisfied
chalyovàv v. saturate
cham n. cheek
chamàhoolya (e) n. pl. jaws
chamikà n. apricot

chami-keràv v. chew
chamikìn n. apricot tree
chamkerav (e) v. chew
chamkerdò (e) adj. chewed up
chàng n. leg, thigh
changàkoo (s) n. womanizer
changò (s) n. leg
char n. grass
char! imp. lick!
charani n. phoenix
charàv (e) v. graze
charàv v. lick
charàv! imp. pasture! graze! take out for
    grazing!
charavàv (s) v. graze
charavnò n. shepherd
chàraybe (sl) sperm
chàrda n. herd
charò n. plate, bowl
charshàfi (s) n. sheet
charyalò adj. green
chatimè adj. assembled
chatìnav v. assemble
chavaldò adj. hit, touched in the head
chavikanò adj. childish
chàvo n. child, son, boy
chavorkanò adj. child's
chavrì n. chicken

chavryakò n. chicken
chay n. daughter, girl
chekàt n. forehead
chekatèste adv. in front
chekìya n. pocket knife
chel n. color pattern
chelava v. color
chemkerèl! imp. chew!
chenès n. chin
chenì n. earring
chentimè n. ground meat
chentinàv v. grind, mince
cherhèn n. star
cherhenyalò n. starry
cheribashì n. mayor
cherpìzava (s) v. treat
cherpizi! imp. treat!
cherta n. line
cheshmyà n. fountain
chetinàv v. read
chetvùrtakoos (s) n. Thursday
chevootsi (s) n. Jew
chib (s) n. tongue
chib n. speech, language
chifitsi (s) n. Jew
chifòot n. Jew
chigarà n. spit
chik n. clay

chik n. mud
chikalò adj. muddy
chikàlyovav v. muddy
chikàt n. forehead
chikìs n. hammer
chikyàs v. thrown away
chikyàv v. steal through, sneak
chilingìr n. farrier
chinàv v. cut, slaughter
chindi-chibengoro n. Albanian [lit. "without a
    tongue]
chingadàv v. scold
chingàr n. argument, quarrel
chingaralò adj. quarrelsome
chingeràva v. punch, pierce through, chop wood
chinìya n. plate
chip n. tongue
chipàs n. something [lyava chipas tikera "I will
    get something to do"]
chiràla adv. long ago
chiriklè n. pl. birds
chiriklò n. sparrow
chishùy (s) n. sand
chocharàv v. empty
chochopì n. plait, tress
chòha n. cloak
chohanò n. vampire
chokàt (s) n. forehead

chon n. moon
choobritsa n. savory
choocharàv v. empty
choochardò adj. emptied
choochì n. tit, woman's breast
choochì del v. nurse
choochì piel v. suck
choochipè n. emptiness
choochò adj. empty
choochò adj. holy, righteous
choochoonyà n. pl. twigs for basket weaving
choochooryà (e) n. icicles
choochvalì n. suckling mother
choochyàte n. suckling
chookàlos n. pestle
chookìzava v. nail, hammer
chookoondòori n. beet (root)
chookòos (s) n. hammer
choolì n. drop
choolyànav v. drip
choomìdav v. kiss
choomìdiba n. kissing
choomidimè adj. kissed
choomidinì n. kiss
choongaràv v. spit
choopinàv v. gnaw
choorì n. braid

choormòot (s) n. moon
chooryalò n. policeman
choozharàva v. clean
chor n. thief
choralò adj. bearded
choràv v. fall
choràv v. steal
choràva (e) v. steal
choràva (s) v. pour
chorbà (s) n. soup
chordanò adj. stolen
chorì n. knife
choribè n. theft
choribì n. theft
choripè n. poverty
chorò adj. poor
chorò n. orphant
choryàl adv. secretly
chovloo n. bachelor
chovròo (s) adj. poor
chulhuya n. pl. stars
chun n. earring
chuy (s) n. girl, maiden
chùyri n. meadow

CSH

cshàd! imp. vomit!

cshadàv n. vomit

cshàdibe n. vomit

cshae! voc. Hey, maiden!

cshaey (srb) n. daughter

cshalù (s) adj. full

csham n. cheek

cshamidinì n. slap

cshamikà n. fig

cshapava v. dig (v)

csharyalò adj. dusty

Cshavàlen! voc. Hey, you!, You, people!

cshavesko cshav n. grandson

cshavesko cshay (s) n. grandaughter

cshavesko cshei (srb) n. grandaughter

cshavò n. son, child, boy [(sl) sòski mocho? i.e.
     soski mo cshavo? "What's doing boy?"]

cshavrì n. chick

cshay (s) n. daughter

cshay n. maiden, daughter, girl

cshel n. measles

cshib n. tongue

cshibalò adj. talkative

cshinàv v. cut, butcher

cshinàv v. tear, break off

cshinàv! imp. cut off!

cshinavàv (s) v. cut off

cshingè! imp. cut up!
cshingeràv v. cut up
cshingeràva v. bore
cshingeryàsla adj. deflowered
cshìpota n. something
cshiv! imp. throw!
cshivàv v. throw
cshivtò adj. thrown
csholàv v. whittle
cshòn n. knife, carving knife
cshon n. moon, month
cshoongàdav v. spit
cshoongàd n. spit
cshoongadimè adj. bespattered
cshoorì n. pocket knife
cshooryalì n. police station
cshooryalò n. policeman
cshoozhòokoos (s) n. type of local hard salami
cshorà n. beard
cshoralò adj. bearded, unshaved
cshoràv v. pour in, serve
cshorcheràva v. spill
cshordò adj. poured out, spilled
cshun n. earring

D
dabà n. beating
dad n. father

dad (srb) n. father
dàda n. older sister
dàde! voc. You dad!
dadèskoro adj. dad's
dàe! voc. You mom!
dakh (s) n. grapes
dàle! (s) voc. You dear!
dalgadès n. waves
dàli n. branch
danakis (s) calf
dànakoos n. tax
dand n. tooth
dandalò adj. jagged
dandàv v. bite
dandèl! imp. bite!
dandelàv v. bite
dandeldò adj. bitten
dàndeliba n. bite
dandinàv v. watch
dant n. tooth
daòoli n. drum
dar n. fear
dar (s) door, gate [pandì oo dar "close the
        door!"]
daràke adj. frightful, dreadful
daranòok adj. cowardly
daràv v. fear
daravàv v. scare

daravdò adj. afraid
das n. Bulgarian
dasikanès adj. Bulgarian
dasikanipè n. Bulgaria
dasikanò adv. Bulgarian
dat (s) n. dad, father
dav v. give
dàvgodi v. advise
davkà pron. this one
dàvkan v. eavesdrop
davòoli n. drum
day n. mother
dayàkoro adj. mother's
dayjo! voc. You uncle!
dayjos n. uncle on the mother's side
de! imp. give!
dèhav v. love, like, enjoy
dèhiba n. love
dehoonòok adj. charming, nice
dek pron. someone
dekhàna adv. sometimes, once upon a time
dekhatàr adv. whence
dekhàte adv. somewhere
dekhòy pron. someone
del n. God, sky, heaven
del n. rain
del n. world
del v. enter

del v. give
delgodì v. remind
delinipè n. madness
delinò adj. mad
delinyòvav v. go crazy
delpesgodì v. remember
demèti n. bundle
demètsi n. bundle
denèdiba n. watching, observation
denedìnav v. watch, follow
dengyaràv v. drive in, shove in
denìs n. sea
dermenzhìs n. miller
deryàv n. sea
deryavestar adj. sea
desh n. ten
desh milyà n. ten thousand
desheftà n. seventeen
deshemès n. floor
deshemìs adv. under
deshohtò n. eighteen
deshoopànch n. fifteen
deshooshòv n. sixteen
dèshto adj. tenth
deshyèk n. eleven
desto n. handle
devèl n. God
dèvi (e) n. spirit, someone with magical power

dèviri (e) adj. upside down
Devla! voc. You God!
devlèskere pògya n. horizon
devlèti n. paradise
devletlùki adj. heavenly
devlikanò adj. divine
dey (srb) n. mother
di part. Isn't it so?
dibès n. day
dìbi n. bottom
diès n. day
diesè adv. daytime
dikh! imp. look! watch!
dikhà soonò v. dream
dikhàv (e) v. look, watch, figure out
dikhàv (e) v. see
dikhàva (s) v. look, watch, see
dìkhiba n. visit
dikhlò n. kerchief
diklò n. kerchief
dilinò adj. crazy, unwise
dilò adj. crazy
dingi n. cart, axis
dis n. town, city
dislyòl v. day breaks
distunò adj. daytime
divès n. day
diyàriya n. diarrhea

diz n. city
diz (pers) n. place
dizootnò adj. city
dizootnò n. citizen
dòda n. sister-in-law
dodàv v. hand over
dolàpi (s) n. cupboard
dolàpi n. water mill
doldò adj. caught
domanò adj. somebody else's
dòmos (s) n. home
doodàv v. hand over
doodòom n. pumpkin
doodoomalò adj. pumpkin
dooimooyalipè n. duplicity
dook n. pain
dookh n. pain
dookhàl man v. it hurts me
dookhala (s) n. pain [moosharoo dookhala
    "I have a headache"]
dookhanì n. hospital
dookhàv soonò v. dream
doom n. back
doomistàr n. back part
doomò n. back
doomòokh n. fist
doonyàs (e) world
door adv. far, away

dooràl adv. far
dooramazhìs n. carpenter
dooripè n. distance
dooroolì n. barrel
dooroolì n. whistle
dooryaràv man v. walk away
dooshàv v. milk
dooshmàn n. enemy
dooshoodòoy n. twelve
dootsìn n. mulberry
doovàki n. veil
dòovar adv. twice
doovàri n. stone fence
doovàri n. wall [of a room]
doovàv v. like
dooy n. two
dooymooyalò n. hypocrite, double-dealer
dooynàs n. world
dòoyshel n. two hundred
doozdìnav v. dress up
doozdìnav man v. dress up myself
dorì n. thread, string
doroos (s) n. yard
dosh n. mistake, guilt
doshàv v. milk
drab n. magic
drab n. medicine
drabalò n. doctor

drabkeràv v. read one's fortune
drakà n. grapes
drakh (s) n. grapes
drakhà (e) n. grapes
drakhèngeri adj. grape
drez n. slander
drom n. road
dromalò (s) n. traveler
dromootnò (e) n. traveler
drosìn n. sunrise
drunkìzava v. jingle
druzhka (s) n. handle
dryàv (e) n. sea
Durnopoli p.n. Edirne
dutsìn n. mulberry
duy (s) n. mother
dyàslis iphoo v. throw on the ground [lit. "gave
    him the ground"—wrestler's term]
dyàva v. give
dyoogèi (s) n. shop, store
dyookyàni n. shop, store

E
e adv. on, upon
Edrelès n. St. George's Day
eftà n. seven

eftàshel n. seven hundred
eftàvardesh n. seventy
ehmimè adj. mixed
ehminàv man v. get involved
ehminàv v. mix
ejèli n. destruction
ek sahàti n. one o'clock
ekàek adv. together
èke adv. right here
ekh n. one
ekhàvar adv. once
ekhvariphàste adv. together
ekipè adv. only
ekledimè adj. pieced together
eklednav v. piece together
eksèri (e) nail
eksìnda n. sixty
èkto adj. first
ekvàsh n. half
Elàda n. Greece
elìnya n. pl. Greeks
emishi (s) n. fruit
ench (s) n. field, cornfield
endanì n. relative
endanipè n. kinship
enyà (s) n. nine
epesèl adv. enough
erèy n. yogurt soft drink

erikin n. plum
erlìdes n. Gypsies living a settled life
ermenìs (s) n. Armenians
ermentsi (s) n. Armenians
esiris n. slave
evènd (e), **event** (s) n. m. winter
evènd (m) winter (n)
evendèskoro adj. winter
ey n. needle
eyàto adj. ninth
eynà (e) n. nine
eynàshel n. nine hundred
eynàvardesh n. ninety
èzeri n. lake
èzeroos n. lake

F

far n. time
fàskya n. wrapper
fastutaya n. peanut
faytòy (s) n. cab
fèra n. gallbladder
fìba n. hairpin
fìlos n. elephant
firaòoni n. Pharaoh, the Gypsy king of the
        Gypsy fairy tales
fitsèri n. officer
flèyta n. flute

fligorna n. cornet
floga n. flame
fooroonjis n. baker
fòota n. apron
fòoti n. apron
foros n. town
frolì n. golden coin
fùsta n. skirt
fustàni n. dress
fuyzàva v. praise

G
gad (e) shirt
gadavàsi (e) adv. so, just so
gadavèske prep. because
gadibòr (e) adv. that much
gajò (e) n. non-Gypsy, foreigner, alien
gajò n. Bulgarian
gajò n. citizen
gajòo (s) n. foreigner
gàlbeya n. pl. golden coins
galì zavàlis v. caress
garà (s) n. railway station
garàv! imp. hide!
garavàv n. hide
garavdò adj. hidden
garàv man v. hide myself
garbò n. sheaf

garèzi n. revenge
gashkanoo kazùi n. bastard
gav n. village
gavèstar adv. peasant, village
gavòodnì (e) n. peasant woman
gavootnò adj. peasant, village
gavorò n. village, hamlet
gechi (e) adv. late
gelè adj. gone
gèmi (s) n. rein
gen n. count
gen n. number
genàv v. count
genàva v. read
gèniba n. reading, counting
ger n. itch
ger n. scabies
geralipè n. baldness
geralò adj. bald
gerdèy (s) n. necklace, girdle
gerdèy n. gutter
gerdey (s) n. washtub
germoosòo n. mouse
gerò adj. wretched
gevechì (s) n. baked vegetables
gevechì (s) n. baking pan
gilì n. song
gilyàbav v. sing

gìlyabe! imp. sing!

gilyabnì n. singer

gìlyaiba n. singing

gilyavàv v. sing

gingyovav v. stretch oneself

giv n. wheat

givesàlo n. dawn

givesè n. daytime

glàbos n. ankle

gledalos (s) n. mirror

godì n. brain

godiàsa (e) adj. wise

godì del v. advise

godisaràv v. think

gogyavèr (e) adj. wise

gomi adj. official

gonò n. bag

gonò (e) n. sack

gonòo (s) n. sack

gooderàva v. sweeten

goodlipè n. sweetness

goodlò adj. sweet

goodlyaràv v. sweeten

goodlyardò adj. sweetened

goodooìn n. quince

goorbèti n. foreigner, stranger

goorgoorìtsa (s) n. f. dove

gooriy (s) n. cow

gooròo (s) n. ox
gooròov n. ox
goroovanò adj. beef, beef meat
gorooveèskaro adj. ox
goroovnì n. cow
gòorti n. yogurt
gootòop n. nape (of the neck)
gopt n. member of the Gypsy "herders" tribe
goshnyà n. dung
gov (s) n. village
goy n. sausage
gozevèr (s) adj. wise
gozì (s) n. mind, brain [telya ti gozi—"to take
       your brain" i.e. surprise]
gozyàsa adv. wisely
gozyavòo manoosh n. wise man
gras n. horse
grasnì n. mare
gredà (s) n. beam
gròzno adj. [grozno manoosh "ugly man"]
grutsi (s) n. Greek
gùluba (s) n. dove
gurbeti n. foreigner, stranger
gurnèta n. clarinet
gyoobètsi n. bellydance
gyoonyòotsi n. wages, one day's pay
gyoorooltìya (s) n. noise
gyoosì n. chest

H

ha! imp. eat!

ha sovel! imp. swear!

habè n. food, bread

habì keràva v. cook food

haètsi n. porch

hahàv! imp. curse!

hahavàv v. curse

hakikàti adj. kind, kindhearted

halaìnka n. housemaid

halavàv v. rinse

halavdò adj. rinsed

halòo adj. bald

halvà (s) n. khalva

halvàs n. khalva

hamoos n. food

hamtsùrus n. strawberry

hanamika (srb) friends, close to one another

handàv v. dig

hanìk n. spring, well

hanikàkeri adj. well, spring

hanjòl v. itch

har adj. deep

har n. ditch

har n. gorge, valley

harabàti adj. untidy

haranìya n. cauldron

haranoo korloo n. thistle

haràri n. measure
haravàv v. scratch
harkòma n. copper, copper kettle
harkomàtar adj. copper
harlò (e) n. bow, fiddlestick
harlò n. sword, weapon
harnèste (e) adj. low
harnipè n. lowland
harnò adj. short
harnòo (s) adj. low, short
harnyaràv v. shorten
harnyovàv v. bring down
haroovàva (s) v. scratch
harvasàra n. synagogue
has n. cough
hasàv v. cough
hashlàva v. graft
haspàs n. rash
hatalì (s) adj. full of money
hav v. eat
havànchis (e) n. mortar
havanchitoos (s) n. mortar
hav holì v. be mad
hav sovèl v. swear
havrì n. chicken
hàvrika n. factory
hay adv. allegedly
hazlùs (s) adj. strong

hebèdes n. saddlebags
hem n. hoop
henamì n. kinsman
henamìka! voc. You matchmaker!
hendò adj. defecated
hents n. strain
her n. m. donkey
heranò adj. donkey
hernì n. f. donkey
hev n. hole
hevlyaràv v. perforate
hevlyardò adj. perforated
hip n. lid
hipalò adj. snub, snub-nosed
hisès n. portion
hlèmeka n. copper
hloinàv v. gush
hlòpka n. bell
hlùchkoba n. hiccup
hluchkònav v. hiccup
hohàv! imp. lie!
hohavàv v. lie
hohavnò n. false
hohayba n. lie
holì n. anger
holimè adj. angry
holtà n. circumference
holyanàv v. be angry

homèr n. dough
hondibà n. groaning
hondìn! imp. groan!
hooharà n. mushrooms (amanitae)
hoohoojà n. twigs
hòola n. stomach
hoolanì n. f. mistress
hoolanò n. m. master
hoolanyàkoro adj. lordly
hoomèr n. dough
hoomeralò adj. dough
hoomimè adj. rumpled
hoominàv adj. rumple
hoor n. bush
hoordò (e) adj. tiny
hoordòo (s) adj. tiny
hoorgyaràv v. break (into pieces)
hòorka n. distaff
hoozharàv v. clean
hor adj. deep
horahanès adv. Turkish style
horahanipè p. n. Turkey
horahanò adj. Turkish
horahày (e) n. Turk
horahnì n. Turkish woman
horahùy (s) n. Turk
hòrata n. word
hòratiba n. speaking, talking

horatìnav v. speak
horipè n. depth
hoy n. anger
hòy v. anger
hoy n. embers
hoynalòo adj. grumpy
hoynalòo adj. sour
hràndav v. plough
hràndina n. ploughing, digging
hùlbookoos (s) n. buttock
hultsìzava v. hiccup
humèr n. yeast
hunzùri n. egotist
hur n. donkey
hurboozoo n. watermellon
hurkàs n. quilted jacket
hùrkolas n. spittle
hùrni n. nostril
hùrpiba n. jumping
hurpìnav v. jump
huyvùya n. animal
huzì n. revenge

I
iblòl adv. last night
ich adv. yesterday
ich i rat adv. the day before
ìchi n. stuffing

igelàv v. carry
ijootnò adj. yesterday's
ikalàv n. take out
ikèr! imp. hold!
ikeràv (e) v. hold
ìkeriba n. behavior
ikestàv v. climb up
ikestilò adj. climbed up
ikhaloo adj. pussy
iklyòvav v. get out
il n. paper
ilìnga n. paper
ilò n. heart
iloo n. heart
inàtsi n. stubborness
indias n. tribe, people
ingàv v. carry
inkyàri n. infidelity
inkyàva v. board
inkyàva naprù v. climb up
ipalàv n. chase out
iràt n. evening
ìriba n. return
irimè adj. returned
irimè adj. turned over
ìrin! imp. return! turn around!
irìnav v. return
irìzava v. turn over

isì v. have
ispelàv v. plant
ispelàv v. shove
ispeldò adj. shoved
ispìn (e) n. lentils
ìsthoiba n. wash
isthovàv v. wash
isthovdò adj. washed
itèmin adv. a little while ago
iv n. snow
ivalò adj. snowy
izbà (s) n. cellar
izprevarizehìs v. outrun
izvìzava v. twist

J
ja! imp. go!
jàmba n. frog
jan! imp. go!
janàv v. know
jàngaliba n. awakening
jangalò adj. awake
jàngalyov! imp. wake up!
jangàlyovav v. awaken
jangavàv v. wake up
jar! imp. wait!
jaràv v. wait
jardò adj. awaited

jàriba (e) n. wait
jav v. go
jendèmì n. hell
jes n. brother-in-law
ji prep. up to [ji ahte "up to here"]
jidikhibnàs n. goodbye
jinèhari adv. later
jìviba n. living
johàpi n. answer
jookèl n. m. dog
jookelorò adj. doggie
jooklè n. doggie
jooklì n. bitch
joongàkoro adj. repulsive
joongalò adj. dirty
joongalò adj. nervous
joongalò adj. quarrelsome
joongalò adj. wicked
joongàv v. loathe
joorapyà (s) n. pl. stockings
joot n. m. Jew
Jootanipè p. n. Israel
jootanò adj. Jewish
jootnì n. f. Jewess
joov n. louse
joovalò adj. lousy
joovèl rig n. left
joovli n. woman

joovlikanò adj. feminine
joovlipè n. femininity
jornì n. offspring from a mixed Bulgarian-Gypsy
    marriage
jorò n. a Gypsy rendered Bulgarian
jorò n. mule
jov n. barley

K

ka part. will [particle forming future tense]
ka pron. because
kafàva n. coffee
kafe n. coffee
kafì n. hen
kafri (s) nail
kahàla kartìndi playing cards
kaìli adj. in agreement with, concordant with
kaili acshòvav v. agree
kaìshi n. belt
kak n. uncle
kakarashka (e) n. jay
kakavì n. cauldron
kakò! (e) voc. You uncle!
kàkoos n. uncle (father's brother)
kakùi n. copper cauldron
kaldarar (srb) n. potmaker
kaldaràshya (e) n. pl. Gypsy nomads
kaldare (srb) n. pot

kaleshrèskoro n. brunette
kalò (e) adj. black, dark
kalò n. crow
Kalò Deryàv p.n. Black Sea
kalòo (s) black
kalòo pepèri n. black pepper
kalpàtsi (s) n. fur hat
kaltsa (s) n. pants, trousers
kalyàl n. darkness
kamàs n. dagger
kamiònoos n. automobile
kan (e) n. ear
kàna adv. when
kanàpi n. string
kandàva (s) n. listen
kangerì n. church
kangeryàko adj. church
kangì n. comb
kanglì (e) n. comb
kanilò adj. bad
kanìzava v. invite
kantarmàs n. bridle
kanzavurì n. hedgehog
kapàtsi n. cover
kàpis (s) drink
kapìya n. scabbard
kapladìnav v. fold
kar n. penis

karakachèy n. members of a Balkan ethnic
    group traditionally living in the mountains

karavàv v. boil

kardaràsha n. nomad Gypsies

karfì n. nail

kàrik adv. where to

karò (e) n. sting

karò (e) n. thorn

kas (s) n. hay

kash n. firelog

kash n. wood

kashkimè adj. squashed, wrinkled

kàshkine! imp. squash!

kashookò adj. deaf

kashtoonò adj. wooden

kàskaro pron. whose

kata-habi n. cook

kàtar adv. from where

kàte adv. where

katlì n. spindle

katùra (s) mule

kavàtsi n. popler

kay! imp. give! [kay mande "give me"]

kay prep. because

kaynàtsi n. spring

kebàpchitoos (s) n. long pieces of grilled
    ground meat

kentra n. joint

kepe n. cap
kepentsyà n. pl. shutters
ker! imp. make! do it!
keràva v. carry
keràva n. build
keravàv v. boil
keràv bootì v. work
keràv hòlta v. go around, circle
keràv man v. pretend
keràva marazàs v. bet
keravav v . boil
ker bootì! imp. work!
kerdì adj. built
kermalò adj. wormy
kermò adj. rotten
kèrmo n. worm
kermoosò n. mouse
kerpedèy n. pliers
keshès n. corner
kezh n. silk
kezhestàr adj. silk
kibir (s) how much? [kibir kurla? (s), kibir kerla?
    (e) "how much does it cost?"]
kibòr adv. as much as
kibrìti n. matches
kichooroos n. tress
kidàv (e) v. gather
kidàva (s) v. gather

kìdiba n. meeting
kilò n. pole [kashoono kilo "wooden pole"]
kinàv (e) v. buy
kindò adj. bought
kinos n. cinema
kinovàv v. buy
kìral n. cheese
kirechi n. lime
kiretsì n. cherry
kirì n. ant
kirivò (e) n. best man
kirmìda n. tile
kirvòo (s) n. best man
kishlò adj. haggard
kisì n. purse, wallet
kitàra (s) n. guitar
kitì (e) how much, how many
klepachì n. eyelids
klìchoos n. key
koch n. ankle
koch n. knee
kochàk n. button
kòchi n. ram
kòchina n. pigsty
kocsh n. knee
kokalò adj. bone
kokalòos (s) n. bone
kòkalos (e) n. bone

kokorchitoos (s) (bot) n. violet
kolà n. automobile
kolìn n. breast
kololòos (s) n. wheel
kololòos n. ring [of a barrel]
kolròo (s) adj. blind
kolròo adj. blind
kolùy n. belt
kòmbos n. knot
kòochibar n. gem
koodìnel v. slander
koodòoni (e) n. bell
kooka n. hook
kòokla n. doll
kookoochìn n. snowflake
kookoodì (e) n. hail
kookoozì (s) n. hail
koolandimè adj. used
koolìn n. breast
kòometsi n. cage
kòona n. cradle, swing
koondoorjìs n. shoemaker, cobbler
koonì n. elbow
kòoniba n. swinging
kooninàv v. swing
koonjoop (e) n. ball, tangle, coil
koonjoopàte (e) adv. in a tangle
koorkò (e) n. Sunday

koorkò n. market
koorkòo (s) n. Sunday
koorkòo (s) n. week
koorshooy n. lead
kooshàv v. pluck
kooshìya n. horse race
kooshiyèti n. racing
kootsìk n. belly
kootsooz n. bad luck
koovilà n. weaving
koovilà tikhoois n. basket weaving
kooy n. elbow
kopanàri n. woodcarver
kopeldatsi n. bastard
kor n. stranger
kor n. member of the Ghor tribe (the largest
    Gypsy tribe in India)
kòra n. bark
kòra n. crust
koripè n. blindness
kòrkorloo adj. alone
korò adj. blind
korò n. rag
koròlyovav (e) v. become blind
koshnichàri n. basket weavers
kosìzava v. mow
kotlyamè n. poison from oxydized copper
kotòr n. piece

kotoralò adj. multicolored
kovalipè (e) n. softness
kovlò adj. soft
kovlò n. sphere
kovròo adj. blind
kozhà (s) n. leather
kris (srb) n. justice [te marel man o kris "may justice kill me!"]
krondìli n. candlestick
krustos n. cross
kuchì n. the rear of a horse or donkey
kurkì (s) n. Sunday
kurlalò adj. greedy
kurleshòos n. tick
kurpì zavà v. mend
kusmèti (s) n. luck
kùti n. insufficient
kutkà adv. here
kutkàres (s) n. nickname of the Gypsies from Mangur Mahle in Sliven
kuzùy (s) n. baby, child
kyooftès (s) n. hamburger
kyootitsi n. stump of a grape vine
kyoshès n. corner

KH
khakh n. armpit
khakh n. scissors

kham n. sun
khamnì adj. pregnant
khamnipè n. pregnancy
khamoos n. food
khan n. stink
khanchìk nothing
khàngeri (s) n. church
khangeryàko adj. church
khanilò adj. bad
khanilipè n. wickedness
khanilès (e) adj. bad
kharlòo n. bow of a fiddle
khas n. hay
khasà v. clean
khasàva n. clean
khayvayà n. animal
khel! imp. dance!
khel! imp. play!
khelàv (e) v. dance
khelàv (e) v. play
khelàva (s) v. dance
khelàva (s) v. play (a game)
khelèl v. shake
khèliba n. dance
kher (s) n. house
kherootnò adj. home
khevliryàv v. drill, pierce through
khidàva v. gather
khil n. butter

khilyardò adj. greasy
khilyavìn n. plum
khilyavin n. plum tree
khilyavinìngeri adj. plum [khilyavinengeri thari "plum brandy"]
khìniba n. tiredness, weariness
khinìlyovav v. get tired
khizim adj. picked, gathered
khom n. sun
khonì n. lard
khònok no one
khool n. shit
khoor n. heel
khoormì n. millet
khoorò n. stallion
khoov! imp. knit!
khoovàv (e) v. knit
khoovàva (s) v. knit
khòoviba n. knitting
khooy (s) n. elbow
khorò n. clay jug
khorò n. pitcher, earthen jug
khosàv (e) v. wipe
khosàva (s) v. wipe
khos! imp. wipe!
khoslò adj. wiped
khoyhalò adj. fat
khoynàlyovav v. get fat

khur (s) n. donkey
khur! intj. wo! whoa!
khuv n. button hole
khuv n. hole
khùy n. elbow

L

la pron. her
lachò adj. clean, pretty
lachshì tì yavìn! good morning
lacshàr! imp. adjust!
lacsharàv v. adjust
lacshardò adj. adjusted
lacshès adv. good
lacshì ti rat! good evening
lacshò (e) adj. good
lacshòo (s) adj. nice, pretty
làdaiba v. load
làdavàv n. load, loading
ladavdò adj. loaded
lahtì n. kick
lahtìdav v. kick
lajà! imp. shame on you!
lajalò adj. shy
lajàv adj. ashamed
lajàv v. be/feel ashamed
lajavò n. shame
lakòo pron. hers

lale n. tulip
lalooroo adj. mute
laluè n. pl. clogs
lamà n. stoning
lama! imp. hit! strike!
lamàda (s) n. flat stone
lamàva v. strike
lamba n. lamp
lamyà n. dragon
lav v. begin
lav v. take
le te yakhà! imp. disappear!
le! imp. take!
lèhooso n. woman in labor
lel n. book
lel n. card
lel n. letter
len n. ditch, mill stream
len n. river
lendò adj. taken
lengèri n. copper baking pan
lèngeri pron. f. their's
les pron. him
lèshi n. corpse
lèskoro pron. his
levavdò adj. naughty
lèvoos n. money
leynàkaro adj. river

Igorù at the end
libnì n. prostitute
likh n. nit
likhalò adj. nitty
lil n. book
lil n. letter
lilalè n. banknotes
lilày n. summer
lilèstar adj. paper
lim n. snot
limalo adj. snotty
limonàda n. lemonade
limòri n. graveyard
lin pron. them
lìndra n. snooze
lindràv v. doze
lingoo (s) pron. their
lìngoorya n. pl. spindel makers
lìniya n. line
lìnta n. lentils
lintàkeri adj. lentil
lis pron. him
lisitsa n. vixen, fox
liskòo pron. his
lizdràv v. shiver
lizdravdò adj. shivering
lòdka n. boat
lohar n. blacksmith

lohar n. the name of the "blacksmiths" Gypsy
   tribe
lokì ti rat! good night!
lokò adj. light
lolipè n. lipstick
lolò (e) adj. red
lolòo (s) adj. red
lolyaràv v. redden
lolyovàv v. blush
lon n. salt
londò adj. salty
longyaràv v. salt
longyardò adj. salted
loobehàri n. "skirt-chaser"
loobipè n. prostitution
loolàva n. pipe
looloodì n. flower
looloogyovàv v. bloom
looloozi (s) n. flower
loongipè n. length
loongo adj. long
loonò (e) n. sickle
loonòo (s) n. sickle
losh n. joy
loshalì n. happiness
loshalò adj. happy
loshanàv v. rejoice
loshanipè n. happiness

loshanò adj. happy
loshazyava v. rejoice
lovàrya n. Gypsy horse traders
lovè n. banknotes
lovè n. money
loy n. spoon
lùvos n. lion
lyàva v. get, start [lyava chipas tikera "start
　　doing something"]
lyàva v. take

LR
lran n. bat
lran n. cane
lròoy n. drum stick
lroy n. spoon
lruy (s) adj. cane
lruy (s) n. bat

M
ma no
machàri n. fisherman
machèsko adj. fish
macshanò adj. fishy
macshèskoro karò n. fish bone
macshò (e) n. fish
macshòo (s) n. fish
madès n. diaphragm (anat.)

magyàrka n. witch
mahàl adj. deservedly
mahàl n. credit
màiba delaying
mainàv v. delay
makhàv n. coat
makhàv v. paint
makhàv v. spread
makhì n. fly
makyaràv v. intoxicate
makyardò adj. intoxicated
makyovàv v. drink one's fill
malì n. goods, merchandise
mami (srb) n. grandmother
mamòoi adv. against
mamòoi (e) across opposite
mamooèste adv. opposite
man pron. me
manè! voc. You mother!
manès n. mahane (Turkish music)
mangàv v. beg
mangàv (e) v. want
mangàva (s) v. want
mangèlpes v. must
mangèn pes v. love each other
mangìn n. treasure
mangìn n. wealth
manginalò adj. rich

mangìs (sl) n. money
mangui n. coal burner
manòok n. boss
manòosh n. man
manooshibè n. kindness
manooshkanò adj. human
mar (srb) v. kill
maràv (e) v. beat
maràv v. knock
maràv v. paste
maràva (s) v. beat
marazà v . bet
marazajìs n. gambler
marazàs v. argue [màker marazàs "don't argue"]
marazàs v. bet
marazàs v. measure against
mardò adj. beaten
marhomè adj. cold
marhònav v. freeze
marhostì n. chill
maribè n. fight
maribè n. war
marime (srb) adj. unclean
marìz (sl) n. beating
marò (e) n. bread
maròo (s) n. bread
marzàl adj. lazy [marzàl man "I feel lazy"]
marzanòok n. lazy person, lazybones

---

mas n. meat
mas n. body
masalò adj. fleshy
masekèste adv. monthly
mashàva n. oak tree
mashkàr n. waist [bookhal man mo mashkàr "my waist hurts"]
mashkàr n. center
mashkar n. cross
mashkàr i rat adv. at midnight
mashkàr o dies adv. at noon
mashkaràl adv. in the middle
mashkarò n. middle
maslìnka n. black olive
matibè n. drunkenness
matò adj. drunk
matòo v. drink
matyovàv (a) v. get drunk
mazès n. cellar
maznoo adj. greasy
me pron. I
me pron. I am
mègar (e) adv. actually, in reality
megdùy n. square
mehanjìs n. innkeeper
mehùy n. bellows
me-karèste (sl) (e), **me-karùsti** (s) It is all the same to me! Big deal! [lit. "It is on top of my penis"]

mel n. grime, dead skin
melalipè n. dirt
melalò adj. dirty
memeli n. candle
men n. neck
menìse n. shoes
menìya n. shoes
menyalipè n. stubornness
menyalò adj. stubborn, tenacious
meràv (e) v. die
meràva (s) v. die
meribè n. death
meshès n. oak
mesùy n. apron
metsìnav v. strain
mezdrimè adj. boneless
mi pron. mine
mi pron. my
mianès n. gruel
mihàni n. bellows
milìna n. cheese strudel
mimòri n. graveyard
minch n. vagina
mindày n. almond
mindjomòoyos n. bootlicker
mìnja (sl) n. vagina
minòota n. minute
minzoohàri n. crocus
mirahchìs n. heir

miriklè n. beads
miriklè n. necklace
miriklì n. cheese pie
misaferlìk n. visit
mishtò adv. well [alyan mishto "welcome"]
misìri n. corn
misìrka n. turkey
mislinàv v. think
mo pron. my
mohtò n. coffin
mohtò n. suitcase
mohtò n. trunk
mol n. wine
Moldovà p.n. Moldova
molnàv v. beg, ask for
molyàri n. wine-merchant, wine producer
molyàvoos n. pencil
mom (pers) tallow
mom n. wax
momeli n. candle
momì n. candle
moo baròo phral n. my older brother
moodàr! imp. kill!
moodaràv v. kill
moodardò adj. dry
moodarè adj. killed
moodarò n. murderer

moodarnò n. murderer
moogì n. elbow
moohanàti adj. careless
moohlyamè adj. mouldy
mook! imp. leave!
mookàv v. leave, postpone
mookàv v. let, permit
mooklò adj. deserted
moolikanò adj. ghastly
moolikanò n. coffin
moolò n. dead man, corpse
moolooklì n. log, stump
mooraiba n. shaving
mooràv v. skin
mooràv! imp. shave!
mooravdè adj. sheared
mooravdò adj. skinned
mooravnò n. barber
moorlòo pron. my
moorsh n. hero
moorsh n. man
moorsh rig n. right-hand side
moorshibè n. heroism, manliness
moorshikanès adj. men's
moort (sl) n. death
mooshkìzava v. stab
moosì n. arm

moosì n. arms, weapons
mooskàri n. calf
mooskarièskoro n. veil
mooskoolis n. muscle
moostàchi v. humiliate oneself
moostàtse n. moustache
mootèr n. urine
mootèr! imp urinate!
mootràva v. piss
mootvàki n. kitchen
mooy n. face
mooy n. mouth
mor! imp. rub!
moràv v. rub
mordò adj. rubbed
morìsko bar n. tombstone
moròo pron. my
morthì n. skin
mortì n. leather
mozì v. breathe
mrazìzava v. hate
mrezhyà n. net
mudìka n. hoe
muna n. golden necklace
murtakoo (s) n. March
murzeliv adj. lazy
mutìzila v. lay (eggs)
myàhoos n. wine bag

N

na no
na-ahàyava v. do not understand
na-anglè adv. forward
naboryamè adj. ill
naboryànav v. fall ill
naboryàsti n. illness
nachimikìn n. fig, fig tree
nadìv v. hope
nadjardò adv. unexpectedly
nafèl n. bad
nak khatàr v. pass through here
nak n. nose
nak n. the tip of the knife
nakandàva v. doesn't listen
nakàriga adv. this way
nakarìk? where to?
nakh n. nose
nakh! imp. pass!
nakhàv v. pass
nakhàv! imp. string!
nakhavàv v. string up, thread
nakhavàv v. transport, carry across
nakhyaràv v. subsist
nakhyaràv v. survive
namangàva v. doesn't want
nàmi n. miracle
nanalyà n. clogs

nanày there isn't

nangi roma n. naked Gypsies [pejorative term for the "naked Gypsies" social group]

nangò adj. naked

nangyardò adj. undressed

nangyòv! imp. undress!

nangyovàv v. undress

nanyaràv v. give a bath

nanyòv! imp. bathe

napalpanè adv. backwards

naprù adv. upwards

nàrchi n. pomegranate

nash! imp. run!

nashalàv v. lose

nashaldòo adj. lost

nashàv v. run

nashchì v. can't

nàshiba n. running

nàshiba v. escaping by running away

nashtì cannot

nashtò n. runaway

nasvalipè n. illness

nasvalò (e) adj. ill, sick

nasvalò n. bad

nasvalòo (s) adj. sick

nasvàlyovav v. get ill

navìzava v. win

nay most

nay n. finger
nay n. nail
nayà n. nail
ne let [avel ne "let him come"]
necipè n. news item
nek v. let
nemlìs adj. humid
nernipè n. soberness
nernò adj. sober
nevò adj. new
nifilyàpa n. bad luck
nijako (e) n. adz [a wood dressing instrument used as a hammer]
nikamàva n. pl. things
nikamàva v. reject
nìkhana adv. never
nilài n. summer
nìsar adv. no way
nìsavo no
noonchìzava v. rest
noot adv. much, a lot
noprù adv. upwards
nuy n. fingernail

O
o art. the [o rom "the Gypsy"]
oblatsì n. cloud

obyadòoski (s) adv. at noon, lunchtime
obyadòoski (s) n. lunch
ochoorava v. cover a horse
odà pron. he
odà pron. sing. you
odalà pron. they
odanà pron. they
odeàlos n. blanket
odiyà (s) pron. she
odyà pron. she
òftika n. tuberculosis
oh pron. they
ohkinàv v. sigh
ohtè adv. there
ohtò n. eight
ohtòshel n. eight hundred
ohtòvardesh n. eighty
ohtyazi adj. torn
ojàkoos n. heart, fire place
okòthar adv. from there
oktò n. eight
omnyazos n. image
onà pron. he
oprè (e) adv. up
oprù (s) adv. up
orahooloo (s) n. boy
orì n. tail
orkèstoorus n. orchestra

othàr adv. from there
otkà adv. there
ov v. be [ov manush "be a man!"]
oy pron. she
o-zaman adv. then, at last
ozhoovyanò adj. left
ozì n. belly
ozì n. heart
ozì n. soul

OO

ooboohotsyà n. circumstances, lit. "works"
    [Sar zhana oobootsya "How are the
    'works' doing?"]
oobootsyà n. things, conditions
oochanàv v. knead dough
oocharàv (e) v. cover
oocharàva (s) v. cover
oocharibè n. roof
oochikeràv v. crumble
oochipè n. height
oochipè n. shadow
oochò (e) adj. high
oochò adj. tall
oochòo (s) adj. high
oochooràva v. cover (a horse)
oocshànav v. winnow, sift
oocsharàv v. close

oocshardò adj. closed
oocshardò adj. covered
oocsharàv v. cover
oocsharibè n. table cloth
oocshdò adj. winnowed, sifted
oodàr n. door
oohkyaràv v. wake up
oohkyàv v. get up
oohlyàv (e) v. comb
oohlyàv! imp. comb!
oohlyàv v. descend
oohiyàv! imp. descend!
oohlyavàv (s) v. comb
oohlyavàv v. take down
oohlyavdò adj. combed
oohlyavdò adj. pulled down
oohtavdò adj. saved
oohtavnò n. saver
oohti! imp. Get up!
oohtyàv v. get up
oojilè v. borrow
oojlipè n. duties
oojlò adj. obliged
oojlyovàv v. run into debt
ooklyòn! imp. all aboard!
ooklyovàv v. mount
oolavàv v. separate

oolavdè adj. separated
oolòov n. shelter
oomàl n. field
oomalyàko adj. field
oomblal n. charcoal
oomblavàv v. hang
oonangi adj. naked
oopral adv. on top
oopràlyavinate n. sunrise
ooprè adv. up
ooproonò adj. upper [ooproono kher "upper
      floor"]
oordiya n. army
oorìtoot! imp. dress!
oorme (srb) n. fates
oorsari n. bear-tamers, the name of "the
      bear-tamers" Gypsy tribe
ooryàv v. dress
ooryàv v. fly
ooryavdò adj. dressed
ooryavzì n. clothing
oosh n. hemp
oosh n. lip
ooshenàv v. knead
ooshendò adj. kneaded
ooshitsi adj. cheap
ooshlò adj. curdled

ooshlò adj. well-risen dough, curdled
ooshlyaràv v. curdle
ooshtàv (e) v. tread
ooshtàv! imp. step!
ooshtavàv (s) v. step
ooshtinkyàrav v. mislead
ooshtinò adj. standing
oostàs kashèskoro n. carpenter
oostàs n. craftsman
oostelizava v. spread out, cover
oostràs n. razor
oozdinàv man v. hope
oozhledinò n. debtor
oozo (srb) adj. clean
oozo adj. clean

P
pabày n. apple
pahajìs adj. expensive
pahajìs n. miser
pàhni n. frost
pahomè adj. frozen
pahòs n. ice
pak n. wing
pakyàr! imp. wrap!
pakyardò adj. wrapped
pakyàv v. believe
pal adv. behind

paladàn behind
palàl adv. behind
palalkoorkò n. Monday
palàtka n. tent
palàtos n. palace
palàv v. fall
pàle adv. again
pàle adv. still [rom, rom, pale rom "Gypsy,
      Gypsy, still a Gypsy!"]
pàlma n. slap
paloonipè n. behind
paloonò adj. the back one, the one behind
paloonthàr adv. at the back, behind
palyà n. floor, pavement
panch n. five
panchayat (srb) council of five
pàncshel n. five hundred
pànda adv. more
pandàv (e) v. tie, lock [pandav vudar "shut the
      door"]
pandàva (s) v. tie
panèri n. pannier, big wicker basket
panì n. water
panilò adj. circled
panlipè n. prison
panlò adj. locked, captured
panshtò adj. fifth
pantaròolya n. fork

pantolyà n. pants, trousers
panyalì n. frog
panyalò adj. water
paoosàv v. freeze
papìn n. goose
papo (srb) n. grandfather
papòo n. old man, grandfather
pàpoo! voc. grandfather!
papòohi n. mushroom
papòor n. reed
papòos n. grandfather
parà n. coin, money
paradoo adj. torn
parahòdoos n. steamship, ship
paramisi n. story, fairy tale
parangòo adj. barefoot
paraskyoovìn (e) n. Friday
paraskyoovìn (e) n. market
parastsivi n. Friday
paravàv v. defeat
paravàv v. split
paravdò adj. torn
parchès n. piece
parès n. money
parèz n. money
parhoodìlis n. burial
parhoomì adj. buried
parikèriba n. gratitude

parila n. dusk [parila iyevin "dawn is breaking"]

paripè n. load

paripè n. sadness, pain [paripè si mànge "I am sad"]

parla n. dusk

parnangòo adj. barefooted

parnanjli adj. barefooted

parnanzì adj. barefooted

pàrniya n. brandy

parno (e) adj. white

parnoo (s) adj. white

pàrnopis n. brandy, rakiya

parò adj. heavy

paromè adj. buried

paronàv v. bury

parordì n. rifle

partsùy n. rag

parus adj. quiet, soft

parvàr! imp. feed!

parvaràv (e) v. feed

parvaràva (s) v. feed

parvaràvman v. eat

paryovàv v. break

pashàl n. relative, close friend

Pashalì n. Easter

pashavrò n. rib

pashè adv. near

pashèste adv. close by
pàshlyov! imp. lie!
pashlyovàv v. lie
pashù adj. close
pashù adv. near, close
pastardinàv v. press down, press
pastarmà n. pastrami
pataselòo adj. cracked
patavè n. puttees
patavì n. puttees
pathoomyà adj. buried
patlazhùy n. eggplant
patò n. rug
patòon n. heel
patragì (vlh) n. holiday
patrìn n. leaf
patsyàva v. believe
patyàv v. believe
pavày n. apple
pavàzes n. the name of the "coppersmiths"
     Gypsy tribe
pavàzya n. polisher, Gypsy tinker
payòom n. heel
pazarizim v. bargain
pazarlutsi n. bargain
pegeràv v. break to pieces
pehlivùy n. wrestle

peìnda n. fifty
peìnda milyà n. fifty thousand
pek! imp. bake!
pekàv v. bake
pekàva v. roast
pekèl v. shine [o kham pekel "the sun shines"]
peklò adj. roasted, baked
pelr n. bellybutton, womb, belly
penàva v. say
pendèh n. hazel nut
penèrka n. basket
penìda n. fifty
penjaràv v. recognize
penjardoonòok n. aquaintance
penjerà n. window
peperòoga n. butterfly; dancing girl in the
    rainmaking dance
per n. womb, belly
per! imp. fall!
peràv v. fall
peravàv n. push over
peravèl n. abortion
perdès n. curtain
peri n. feather
perì pron. hers
perodrùshka n. pen
perorì n. bee

pèrsi adv. before
pèrsi n. last year
peryas-kerava v. talk
pesh adv. on foot, walking
petalonàv v. dress with horseshoes
petaloos (s) n. horseshoe
pètalos (e) n. horseshoe
pètoora n. strudel leaf
pevtsi n. Thursday
piav v. drink
pihìn! (e) imp. breathe
piìs v. drink
pikò (e) n. shoulder
pikòo (s) n. shoulder
pilà n. file
piltsèyla v. marry
pinangò (e) adj. barefooted
pingò (sl) adj. crooked
pinjaràv v. know, be aquainted with
piràv (a) v. go, perish
pireybi n. copulation
pireylapis n. love
pirì n. ceramic pot
pirìngoro n. pot maker
piroostsì n. trivet, grill
pirootnò n. traveler, bum
piryakerò n. pot maker
piryamlòo n. lover

pishoom n. flee
pishòt n. bellows, waterskin, wineskin
pisìka n. cat
piskyòoy n. tassel
pistolètoos n. gun
pitav n. honesty
piyàv v. drink
plakomè adj. pressed, squashed
plakonàv v. press down
plamnìselo v. caught fire
plamniselo v. start burning
platòos n. cloth
platsìzava v. pay
platsizì! imp. pay!
plàyna n. mountain
plìtka n. plait
plìtoo n. shallow
plivinàv v. swim
plùhoos n. rat
podày zavà v. hand, hand over
podènav v. put on shoes
podpirisalma v. lean against
pogyà n. skirt, dress
poharì adv. soft, slow
pohtàn n. cloth, material
pokìn! imp. pay!
pokinàv v. pay
Polinà p. n. Istanbul

polokès adv. slow
polr n. stomach
polryà n. pl. guts
pomàtsi n. Christian converted to Islam
ponedèlnikoos n. Monday
pookeràv v. inflate, bloat
pooknì n. boil
pooknì n. wound
poomarè adj. private
poongaràva v. know
poonjàr! imp. Guess! Recognize!
pooranèste adj. second-hand
pooranò adj. worn out
pooranò koorkò (e) n. Sunday
pooranòo adj. old
pooranòo manoosh n. old man
pooranyàv v. grow old
poorèi adj. old
poorèi roomì n. old woman
poorloo n. thigh
pooroomalò (e) adj. spiced with onions
pòoshko n. rifle
pooshoom n. flea
pooteràv v. untie
por n. plume, feather
por n. tail
poravàv v. stretch
Poravdì p.n. Bosphoros [literary: "The crack"]

porh (srb) n. belly
porl n. gut
porl n. intestine
porl n. nipple
pornangòo adj. barefooted
porya n. pl. guts
porya n. pl. tails
posavàv v. pierce
poshi n. sand
poshom n. wool
postelizi! imp. spread out!
postey (e) n. shoe
postùya (s) n. pl. shoes
pothàva v. say
potinyà n. pl. shoes
pràgoos n. threshold
pràhos n. dust
pral (sl) pal, friend
pralisko cshow n. nephew
prandemè adj. married
prastàv (e) v. run
prastàva (s) v. run
prehoratinàv v. foretell
prepàv v. look like
presovàv v. sleep over
prètoora n. municipal building
proot n. bridge
propinàv v. lean against

prosizavà v. beg
punjaravàlis v. become fat
pùpka n. pimple, blotch
purlènta n. silk headkerchief
purnangòo (s) adj. barefooted
purnanzì adj. barefooted
putèka n. path, track
puy n. water
pyàva v. drink

PH
phabaràv v. light up, kindle
phabùy n. apple
phagàv v. break
phagàva v. break down
phagha n. break
phaglyàrav v. change money
phakh n. wing
phand! imp. close! shut!
phàndiba n. prison
phandlò n. prisoner
pharastsivì n. Friday
pharavdò adj. split
pharavdò adj. torn
pharès adv. slowly
pharipè n. weight
pharò adj. heavy

phen n. sister
phenàv v. answer
phenàv v. say
phepya n. aunt
phèr! imp. fill up!
phèrdo adj. full
pheryàva v. gain weight
pheryovàv v. become fat
phikò (e) n. shoulder
phikò n. support
phikòo (s) n. shoulder
phimipe n. craftiness
phiràv v. go, perish
phiràv (e) v. walk
phiràva (s) v. walk
phirdòo n. walk
phirindòs adj. walking
phivlò n. widower
phoo n. ground
phoocsh! imp. ask!
phoocshàv v. ask
phoodàv v. blow
phoode! imp. blow!
phooklò adj. filled up
phookni n. boil
phoom n. pus
phoorano adj. old

phoordoo adj. dusty
phoos n. straw
phoosano adj. straw
phootèr! imp. open!
phooterdò adj. opened
phoov khelèl n. earthquake
phoov n. land
phoovyalò n. peasant
phorò n. abdomen
phòsaiba n. shooting pain
phosavdò adj. convenient
phov n. eyebrow
phovà n. eyebrow
phral n. brother
phralikanò adj. brotherly
phralipè n. brotherhood
phub n. pus

R
ràdika n. turnip
rahvàni n. trot
raklì n. non-Gypsy girl
raklò n. non-Gypsy boy
raktèr! imp. spend the night!
rakyàsa n. evening time
rakyàsa n. night time
rakyòvav v. grow dark
randàv v. reap

randimè adj. reaped
randlò adj. shaved
ràrolyov! imp. be dumb!
ràròlyovav v. grow dumb
rarorikanès adv. mimicking
rarorò adj. dumb
rashày (e) n. east orhodox priest
rashhanì n. priest's wife
rastìri n. blacksmith's spot
rastìri n. forge
rastsi n. fireplace
rastsirì n. fireplace
rat (srb) n. blood
rat adv. during the night
rat n. evening
rat n. night
ratkeràv n. spend the night
ratsyàsa adv. night time
ratvalilò adj. bloody
ratvalò adj. bloody
ratvalyaràv adj. cover with blood
ravalì n. sack
ràvalos n. sack
ravàv man v. complain
ravìn! imp. dig!, poke around!
ravinàv v. plough
rayà n. twigs for basket weaving
razprèyzila n. tale

rèbroos n. rib
res! imp. catch up with!
res! imp. welcome!
resàv v. catch up with
resàv v. reach
resàv v. ripen
resàv v. welcome
resavàv v. complete
resavàv v. supply
resavdò adj. supplied
reshètka n. sieve
rèshtos n. sieve
restò adj. welcome
revizava v. scream
rez n. vineyard
rich n. bear
richnì n. she-bear
richnuanò adj. bear
ricshì n. bear
ricshìy n. bear
rig n. side
rikanoonò adj. dog's
rikonanò adj. canine
rikonò n. dog
ring n. angroostì
rinì n. file
rinimè adj. filed

rininàv v. file
ritsìna n. violin string wax
rivìn! imp. plough!
robì n. slave
ròdav v. seek
roi n. spoon
ròiba n. cry
ròoy n. drumstick
rom n. Gypsy
rom n. Gypsy husband
rom n. husband
romanipè n. Gypsy way, Gypsy tradition
romanò adj. Gypsy
romnì n. Gypsy wife
romnì n. Gypsy woman
romni n. wife
roohoozìna (s) n. rush-mat , straw mat
roomi n. woman
roop n. silver
roopoovalò adj. silver
roov n. wolf
roovanò adj. wolf
roovnì n. she-wolf
ròoy n. drumstick
rooy n. stick
rov! imp. cry!
rovàv (e) v. cry

rovàva (s) v. cry
rovavnò adj. tearful
rovìlapis adj. complaining
rovlì n. club
rùgya n. misery
rugyalò adj. miserable
rus n. vineyard
rushày (s) n. east orthodox priest
rushùy n. priests
ruy n. stick
ruz n. vineyard

S
sa adv. always
sabàlen adv. at daybreak
sabàlen n. morning
sàbya n. sabrer
sadè only
sahati dui n. two o'clock
sahàti n. clock
sahàti n. hour
sahàtsi n. clock
sahàtsi n. hour
saidìnav v. respect
sakatì adj. lame
sakatì adj. onehanded, crippled

salchì n. branch
salchinyalò adj. branchy
saldàtsi n. soldier
salò n. brother-in-law
sandùtsi n. coffin, trunk
sànkya n. sled
sanò adj. thin
sanopè n. thinness
sanùy n. sandals
sanyovàv v. thin out
sanzì n. board
saòoni (a) n. soap
sap int. how
sap like
sap n. m. snake
sapanò adj. snake
sapnì n. f. snake
sar as
sarànda n. forty
sar int. how
sar sinyàn? how are you?
saranda milyà n. forty thousand
sarorò all
saskyarav v. heal
saskyardò adj. cured
saskyarno n. doctor
saskyovàv v. get cured

sasooè! voc. You Mother-in-law!
sasòoy n. mother-in-law
sastaryàv v. heal
sasti n. hat
sastipè n. health
sastò adj. healthy
sastò whole
sàstra n. iron
sastrakàne parès n. coins
sastras (s) n. iron
sastrò (e) n. father-in-law
sastròo (s) father-in-law
sasùy n. mother-in-law
sauzì n. board
savatoos (s) n. Saturday
sàvatos (e) n. Saturday
savayà n. basket
savè what
savì what
sàvoro all
savutoo n. Saturday
sàydiba n. respect
saydimè adj. respected
sekanà always
sèko every
sel all
sem v. to be
sèmi n. seed

senya adj. shady
sèpniba adj. startling
sepnìnav v. start, be startled
sergìya n. stall, stand
sèsi n. voice
sèviba n. thunder
sevinal v. lightning/thunder strikes
sevinel v. lightning strikes
sèvli n. basket
sevlyà (vlh) n. baskets
si v. are [odana si "they are"]
si pron. is
sichkoma pron. all
sig n. speed
sigò already
sìgo adj. fast
sigòo already
sigòo adj. fast
sigyaràv v. hurry
sìgyariba n. haste
sigyarindòs adv. hurriedly
sìiba n. sewing
sikavàv v. point
sikavàv v. teach
sikavdò n. learned, erudite
sikavnò n. teacher
sìkliba n. study, learning
siklò adj. accustomed
siklò adj. trained, educated

siklyovàv v. study
silkyàva v. study, learn
silyàva n. pliers, tongs
sim v. am
simpoori n. sulfur
sinhanì n. lioness
sinhanò adj. lion
sinhày n. lion
sinjiri m. chain
sinti (srb) n. people
sinyàm v. are [amin sinyam "we are"]
sinyom v. am
sir n. garlic
siryalò adj. onioned, spiced with onion or garlic
sivàv v. sew
sivdò adj. tailored
sivrì n. hammer
Sivrìkes n. Christmas
siya tooevìn n. prune
siynì v. turn blue
siyòo adj. blue
skafidì n. kneading-trough
skami n. chair
skàra n. grill
skavzì n. trough for bread kneading
skomi n. chair
skomyànoos n. chair
skootsìzi adj. dark

slàbo adv. weakly, feebly
sloochisàlo n. happening, occurance, event
smenìdas n. change
snàga n. body
so instead
so what
soìba n. sleep
sokàtsi n. street
somnakày n. gold, gold ring
sonooyzava (s) v. dream
soo n n. needle
sookàlchitoos n. suckling lamb
soolavàv v. clean, sweap
soong n. smell
soongàv v. smell
soonò n. dream
soonòdikhav (e) v. dream
sooslò adj. raw, wet, moist
sooslyaràv v. wet
sooslyardò adj. wet
sootò v. sleep
soov n. needle
soozàv v. itch
sosì int. what is the matter?
soskòotoo conj. because
sostèn n. underpants
sov v. sleep
sov! imp. sleep!

sovàlka n. shuttle
sovavnò adj. sleepy
sovel n. oath, curse
sovèl n. vow
sovlyadav v. take an oath, swear
sovlyaràv v. sleep over
sovnà n. gold
sovnalò adj. golden
sòvra all
soyna n. sleep
spanakoos n. spinach
sras n. iron
srast n. iron
srasta n. iron
srastoonò adj. iron
srastrakàni n. iron
stadì n. hat
stadìk n. cap
stanoos n. loom
stiptsàr n. miser
stòka n. goods, ware, merchandise
stoopì n. toe
stràha n. yard wall
straine (srb) n. strangers
strakìna n. pot
strelìzava v. shoot
stròngya n. providence

strùmno adj. steep
stùlba n. ladder
suìzi v. sow
sunòoyzava v. dream
supnimè adj. tripped
supninàv v. trip
sùrbi n. Serb
surnà n. deer
sùvi n. wicker basket
suy adj. grey
svetkavitsa n. lightning
svitka n. spark
syam (s) sing. are [toomin syam "you are"]
syan (s) pl. are [too syan "you are"]
syànka n. shade
syànka n. shadow
syòorgyòoy n. diarrhea

SH
shah n. cabbage
shamdàni n. priest
sharàs n. don't
sharàv v. praise one's own self, show off
shày v. can
shebètsi n. monkey
shedès n. bottle

shèhya n. belongings
shèhya n. clothes
shel n. one hundred
shelò n. rope
shelyà n. bran
sheràand n. pillow
shernangò adj. bareheaded
sherò n. head
sheroonò adj. chief
sheynà n. sled
shil n. cold, chill
shiltès n. bed spread
shing n. horn
shìnilis adj. lively
shish n. spit
shishè n. bottle
sho n. six
shòldav v. whistle
shoodri n. cold (with a runny nose)
shoodrò (e) adj. cold
shoodròo (s) adj. cold
shoodryalyàv v. chill
shoodryovàv v. catch a cold, catch a chill
shoojaràv v. clean
shook n. beauty
shookàr adj. beautiful
shookàr adj. good
shookaripè n. beauty
shookipè n. drought

shookò adj. dry

shookò adj. lean

shookyaràv v. dry

shookyovàv v. dry out

shoolàv! imp. sweep!

shoolavàv v. broom, sweep

shoolavdò adj. swept (off)

shoon! imp. listen!

shoonàv v. hear

shoondò adj. famous

shoongòori (bot.) (e) n. carob, carob pot,
    locust bean

shoonyovàv v. become famous

shoot n. vinegar

shootlò adj. sour

shootlòo adj. sour

shootlyahà n. sorrel (bot.), sour dock (Rumex)

shoovàl n. broom

shoovàr n. halter

shoovlilò adj. swollen

shoovlò adj. fat

shoovlyovàv v. swell

shoozharàv v. clean

shoozhipè n. cleanliness

shoozhò adj. clean

shòro n. head

shosès n. highway

shoshnì n. doe-rabbit

shoshoèskoro adj. rabbit

shoshòy (e) n. rabbit
shoshùy (s) n. rabbit
shov n. six
shovàrdesh n. sixty
shòvshel n. six hundred
shovtò adj. sixth
shtapka n. step
shtapkèr! imp. step!
shtapkeràv v. step
shtar n. four
shtàrshel n. four hundred
shtòopos n. garbage
shul bresh n. century
shurnangòo adj. bareheaded
shùya n. bran

T
tabàhna n. leather shop
tabàk n. leather
tabèla n. shop sign
tablàti n. backgammon
tablyàv v. burn
tagavàv v. drown, choke
tahtabitsa n. bedbug
tahtày n. (e) glass, cup
tahtùy n. (s) cup
taksiràti n. punishment
takyaràv v. warm up

takyovàv v. warm myself
talàl vastès n. bribe
talìga (s) n. cart, wagon
talòl adv. down
tamar n. member of the "ironsmiths" Gypsy tribe
tan n. place, land
tanàli n. playground
tang adj. narrow
tangipè n. narowness
tangyàrav v. narrow
taralèzhoos n. hedge hog
tarashtàv v. steal
tarashtù stealing
taròo adj. hot, hot taste
tasavàv v. choke
tasavàv v. strangle
tasavdò adj. drowned
tasavdò adj. strangled
tashtìnav v. boil
tashtìnav v. overflow
tasià n. tomorrow
taslyivàv v. choke, drown
tàsos n. copper bowl
tasyà adv. tomorrow
tasyà ki rat tomorrow night
tataryàv v. heat up
tàtin! imp. taste!
tatìnav v. taste

tatipè n. warmth
tàto (sl) coffee [lit. "a hot one"]
tatò adj. warm
tatipè n. warmth
tatòjiya (sl) n. coffee house owner
tatòo adj. hot
tatyovàv v. warm
tavà n. baking pan
tavà n. pan
tavànoos n. attic
tavànoos n. ceiling
tavàva v. wash
tavdala adj. leaking, dripping
tavdanilò running, dripping
taynè! imp. Shut up! Be silent!
te if
te to
teatroos n. theater
techènie n. current, river current
techènie n. draft
telàl adv. underneath
telalyakhà n. suspicion
telè adv. down
telì adv. down
telonì soste n. drawers
teloonipè n. lower part [as for instance the
     pants of a sweat suit are the "teloonipè" of
     a sweat suit]
teloonò adj. low

telyovàv v. bend down

temenòoga (bot.) n. violet

tepès n. mount

terasùslis v. catch up with

terdindòs adv. standing

tereziyà n. scale

tèrgyovav v. stand

terì pron. yours

ternèngoro adj. youthful

ternipè n. youth

ternò (e) adj. young

ternòo (s) adj. young

ternyòl young looking

terò pron. yours

teryava v. stay

tetikèste v. be on the alert

tetìki n. tenseness

tetivà n. string of an instrument

tetkàkoro n. cousin on the aunt side

tetràzi n. Wednesday

tevekeliès adv. in vain

tevlès n. dregs

tevlès n. sediment, mud

teyunì sostè n. drawers

tìguri n. tiger

tìhoo adj. soft [po-tìhoo kerperyàs "speak more
    softly"]

tikhoois n. basket weaving

tilya mozì v. breathe, take breath

---

tlàkos n. slime
tochiloos n. touchstone
tokàs n. clasp, buckle
too pron. sing. you
tòohla n. brick
toojàri n. merchant
tookè for you
toomìn pron. pl. you
tooman pron. you
toomarò pron. yours
toomaròo pron. your
Tòona p. n. Danube
toonyà n. trouble
tooryàl v. alongside of, around
tooryànav v. circle, tour
tooryalìste adv. circling around
toot n. cornet
toot n. clarinet
toot n. milk
toot pron. you
toovni n. she-wolf
tooyavìn n. plum
tòpa n. ball
torò pron. yours
toròo pron. your
torlòo pron. sing. yours
totasìya n. the day after

tòtasya n. the day after
tovàv v. wash
tovàv v. put
tovèr n. ax
tràdav v. drive
trèbinal v. must
trìnshel n. three hundred
trashanàv v. get scared
trastà n. bag
tren n. train
triànda n. thirty
trin n. three
trivònos n. saw
triyànda milyà n. thirty thousand
tromàv v. dare
troodovàtsi n. work squad soldier
trooshò n. cross
troosh n. thirst
trooshalò adj. thirsty
trooyàl prep. around, about
trooyanyàv v. go around
trubà n. pipe
tuktìnav v. stuff up, jam
tukumyè n. horse gear
tuvryazì (s) adj. sober
tùzhno adj. sad
tyàlos n. body

TH

thabaryàv v. light, burn
thabatyàv v. burn
thabila v. burn
thablyòl n. burn out
thablyovàv v. burn
thagar n. king
thagaripè n. kingdom
thagarnì n. queen
thagarutnò adj. king's, regal
than n. bed
than n. den
than n. place
thanootnò adj. local
thanootnò adj. settled down
thar n. molar tooth
tharav v. light
tharì n. brandy, fruit brandy
tharoo adj. hot, spicy
thav n. thread
thàvdav v. run, flow
them n. state
themootnò adj. state
thoodvalò adj. milk
thoolipè adj. thickness, fatness
thoolyovàv v. thicken, gain weight
thoot n. milk

thoov n. smoke
thoov n. tobacco
thov n. thread, string
thovàv v. put
thovava v. wash

TS
tsamtsàlya n. eyelashes
tsàra n. covered wagon
tsàra n. Gypsy camp tent
tsaròoy n. pigskin sandal
tsarunò adj. Gypsy camp style
tsedèl n. fireplace
tsèpezi! imp. chop!
tsèrha n. rug
tsezelyaslis oocshoroo v. hit the mark
tsibrìava v. shine
tsìbriba n. light
tsibrìnel v. shine
tsìdav v. haul
tsìdav v. pull
tsìdav v. pull ahead, start on my way
tsìdiba n. pulling
tsìdiba n. weight
tsidimè adj. measured
tsidimè adj. pulled

tsidinè v. got started
tsigara n. cigarette
tsihà n. rheumatism
tsihàn n. frying pan [sushtosyan maznoo
    tsuhani "you are like a greasy
    frying pan"]
tsihàni n. frying pan
tsikìnda n. nettles
tsiknedèr adj. smaller
tsiknipè n. childhood
tsiknò adj. small
tsiknò màsek n. February
tsiknyà n. smell of burning
tsikooroo ahgooshtoo n. small finger
tsikooroo zhookel n. puppy
tsikurì n. kitten
tsìla n. pile
tsimbàli n. cymbal
tsinàva v. buy
tsinkyaràv v. shorten
tsinkyovàv v. diminish
tsìpa n. membrane, envelopment
tsìral n. cheese
tsìrka n. circus
tsirkajìs (s) n. clown
tsirkajìs n. circus actor
tsirmoo n. worm
tsìroos n. day

tsìroos n. weather
tsìros n. time
tsitsanò n. tomcat
tsitsày (e) n. cat
tsitsayàkoro adj. cat's
tsitsèli n. poison
tsìtseliba n. poisoning
tsitselìnav v. poison
tsitsey (e) n. cat
tsitsùy (s) n. cat
tsiyava n. plum tree
tsuklòs n. glass
tsurhà n. fleecy rug
tsvyàtoos n. color

V

va yes
vàda n. mill-stream, ditch
vadàva (s) v. lift
vàker! imp. say! tell!
vakeràv (e) v. say
vakerava (s) v. say
vàkeriba n. say
vakùti n. time
vakùtsi n. time [boot vakùtsi nàkistoo "a lot of time passed"]
valyamè adj. tumbled
valyànav v. tumble

var (vlh) time [efta var-desh "seven times ten"
     i.e. seventy]
vardò n. cart
varènjak even
vàresavo some
vàreso n. something
vàrya n. sledgehammer
vas conj. because of
vas n. hand
vastèskeri n. pl. gloves
vàzdav v. lift
vàzdav vas v. raise a hand [to hit]
vazdimè adj. elevated
vehtoshàre n. old clothes dealer, second-hand
     dealer
vesh n. forest
vesh n. mountain
veshinò adj. forest
veshootnò adj. forest
veshtahàr n. forester
vestò adj. healthy
vìholas n. egotist
vìnga (e) n. hearth, blacksmith's hearth in the
     ground
vint n. bolt
vitsa n. family tree
vitsa n. vine
vlahyà n. pl. Gypsy spindel-makers

vlàstsi (s) n. Romanians
vogi n. soul
voodàr n. door
vòonda n. horseshoe
voordò n. cart
vooshtà n. lips
vosh (pers) n. forest
voy pron. she
vrahnyànav v. exhaust oneself [vrahnyanav
     tatipnastar "get exhausted from the heat"]
vràsi n. boil over, boil
vràsi n. weld, welding
vrehòolka n. storm
vrùhoos n. tip, peak
vrutsa n. bristle
vtòrnikoos n. Tuesday
vùrba n. willow
vurdò n. cart, wagon
vurdon (pers) n. cart
vurtsi mi puy (s) n. whirlpool [lit. "water twisting]

Y
yag n. fire
yahvalò adj. deserted
yahvalò v. ravage
yahvalyovàv v. become deserted
yak n. fire

yakh n. eye
yakhalì cshiyav v. wink
yakhalòo cshelà v. wink [lit. "cast an eye"]
yalò n. crude, raw, rough
yar n. file
yardàn n. help, favor
yàstagachi n. low round dining table
yavàlis butsèti v. hire
yavèn n. dawn
yavìn adj. early
yavinàte adv. at daybreak
yavinàti n. dawn
yek n. one
yekìsti adv. together
yerdìles n. locals [the name the Sofia Gypsies
        give to themselves]
yeshìl adj. green
yòla n. violin
yooklòotsi n. wall wardrobe
yoolòo n. liver
yoolròo (s) n. liver
yoov n. snow
yoy pron. she

Z
zabaralyàv v. become rich
zàbava v. sing
zagradimè n. fence

zàhodoos n. toilet
zalavàv jag v. build a fire
zamàn adv. then
zanaèthi n. craft
zanayàthi n. craft
zanayètsi n. occupation
zàpekoos n. constipation
zaplatà n. wages
zàprezi! imp. stop!
zaprìzava v. stop
zar adj. without hair
zar n. dice
zaràri n. loss
zaronàv v. feeze
zavet n. lee, shelter from the wind
zelèno adj. green
zen (e) n. stirrup
zen n. saddle
zenginì n. stirrup
zepìzava v. stare
zerdelin n. apricot
zes n. day
zikarlòo adj. small
zikarui adj. small
zikoorlòo m. small
zis n. city
zis n. market place
zivisù adv. midday time

zòmka that much
zoomì (e) n. dish
zoomì n. soup
zoorlà n. snout, muzzle
zor n. strength, power
zoralèste adj. strong
zoralò (e) adj. powerful, tough, healthy
zoralòo (s) adj. strong
zoràlyovav v. get strong, toughen
zuntyà n. kick with hind legs
zvyàros n. beast
zyan n. loss
zyoombyòol n. hyacinth

ZH

zhàmba n. frog
zhambazi n. horse traders
zhamootrò n. son-in-law
zhanava v. know
zharàv v. stay, wait
zhatsin! imp. buy!
zhemì n. glass
zhèmi n. window
zhèzhbya n. Turkish coffee pot
zhìns n. family, clan
zhìto n. wheat
zhivàkos n. mercury, quicksilver
zhoo n. flee

zhookél n. dog
zhooklanòo adj. dog
zhoovalòo adj. lousy
zhoovèl n. woman
zhoràpe n. stocking
zhov n. barley
zhov n. grain
zhow n. barley
zhultòo adj. yellow
zhush n. brother-in-law
zhushtuy n. sister-in-law

ENGLISH-GYPSY DICTIONARY

A

abdomen n. phorò
abortion n. peravèl
absent adj. bejìti
absent-minded adj. azdimè ["my brain is not in its place" mi gozì nanùy thanèsti]
accustomed adj. siklò
actually mèger
adjust v. lacsharàv
adjust! imp. lacshàr!
adjusted adj. lacshardò
advise v. godì, del, dàvgodi
adz n. nijako (e), tesla (s)
afraid adj. daravdò
afternoon n. kuy khorichka **early afternoon**; avsha misti **late afternoon**
again adv. pàle
against prep. mamòoi
agree v. gotovozava (s)
agreed upon adj. kaìli
airplane n. aeroplànoos
Albanian n. chindi-chibengoro [literary: "with a cut tongue"]
a little while ago itèmin

---

alive adj. jivdò
all sòvra, sel
all adv. sàvoro
all aboard! imp. ooklyòn!
allegedly adv. hay
almond n. mindày
alone adj. kòrkoro
alone adv. kòrkorlòo
alongside of adv. tooryàl
already adv. sigòo, sigò
always sekanà
always sa
am v. sem, sinyom, sim
am pron. me
angel n. àngelas
anger n. holì
anger v. holanàv
angry adj. holyamè, holimè
animal n. huyvùya, khayvayà, huyvùy
ankle n. glàbos
another adj. avèr
another place adv. avrehtè
answer n. johàpi
answer v. phenàv
ant n. kirì, kir
anvil n. amunì
apple n. phabùy, aphai, pabày, pavày
apricot n. chamikàr, chamikà, zerdelin

apricot tree n. chamikìu, chamikìn
apron n. footi, mesùy, fòota
aquaintance n. penjardoonòok
are v. sinyàm [we are "amin sinyam"]
are v. syan [you are sing. "too syan"]
are v. syam [you are pl. "toomin syam"]
are v. si [they are "odana si"]
argue v. marazàs [don't argue "màker marazàs"]
arrive v. avàva
arm n. moosì
Armenians n. ermentsi
armpit n. khakh
arms n. moosì
army n. oordiya
around adv. trooyàl
arrange v. bichalàv
as sar
ascend v. ooklyovàv
as far as adv. chak
a smiling man asanòo mànoosh
as much as adv. kosòm
how much kibòr
ashamed adj. lajàv
Asia Minor p.n. Anatoliyà, Anatolàte
ask for v. molnàv
ask v. phoocshàv
ass n. bool
assemble v. chatìnav

---

assembled adj. chatimè

at daybreak adv. sabàlen, yavinàte

at last adv. o-zaman

at least adv. bàrema [if he at least was a [real] man "barema manoosh te avel"]

at lunch obyadooski

at midnight adv. mashkàr i rat

at noon adv. mashkàr o dies

at the back paloonthàr

at the end adv. agorù, Igorù

attic n. tavànoos

aunt n. àla, phepyà

automobile n. kolà

awaited adj. jardò

awake adj. jangalò

awakening n. jàngaliba

a while n. harikà, harichkà [Sit for a while! "Besh harichkà!"]

ax n. tovèr, bràdva

axis n. dingì

ayran [yogurt drink] n. ayrùi, erèy

B

baby n. kuzùy

bachelor adj. bi-romnyàkoro

bachelor n. chovroo, chovloo

backgammon n. tablàti

back n. doom, doomò, doomòo

back part n. adj. doomistàr
backwards adv. napalpanè
bad adj. kanilò, khanilò
bad adj. bi-lachò, gonò, trastà
bad luck n. nifilyàpa, kootsooz
bad n. nafèl, nasvalò
bake v. pekàv
baked adj. peklo
baker n. fooroonjìs, abèjiya
baking pan n. tavà, gevechì
balcony n. balkòy
bald adj. bi-balèngero, halòo, halòogeralò,
    bìbalìngu
baldness n. geralipè
Balkans adj. Balkàn
ball n. tòpa
bank n. bànka
banknotes n. ilìnga parès, lilalè, lovè
baptism n. àyos
baptize v. boimlis
barber n. mooravnò
barefoot adj. parangòo, pinangò, parnandzli,
    pirnangò, pornangòo, parnanzì
bareheaded adj. shurnangòo, shernangò
bargain n. pazarlutsi, pazarizim
bark [of tree] n. kòra
bark n. bashàv
bark v. bashàv, bashalàv

barley n. zhov, jov
barn n. avlìn
barrel n. dooroolì
basket n. penèrka, savayà, sèvli, sùvi
basket maker n. koshnichàri
basket weaving v. tikhoois
basket weavers n. kaldaràshes
bastard n. kopeldatsi, gashkanoo kazui
bat n. lran, lruy
bathe! imp. nanyòv!
be angry v. holyanàv
be mad v. hav holì
be on the alert v. tetikèste
be scared v. daràv
be silent! imp. taynè!
be v. ov [be a man! "ov manush"]
beads n. miriklè
beam n. gredà
beans n. bòboos
bear n. rich, ricshìy, ricshì
bear v. benà, bianàv
bear tamers n. oorsari
beard n. cshorà
bearded adj. choralò, cshoralò
beast n. zvyàros
beat v. maràva, maràv
beaten adj. mardò
beating n. dabà, màris, marìz (sl)

beautiful adj. shookàr
beauty n. shookaripè, shook
because conj. soskòotoo, gadavèske
because of prep. vas
become deaf v. kashookinàv
become deserted v. yahvalyovàv
become famous v. shoonyovàv
become fat v. punjaravàlis, pheryovàv
become hungry v. bokalyàv
become rich v. barvilivàva, zabaralyàv
bed n. than
bed spread n. shiltès, boohlyaribè
bedbug n. tahtabitsa
bee n. berorì, berolì, booriya
beech n. book
beef n. gooroovanò
beer n. bìra
beet root n. chookoondòori
before adv. andò, pèrsi, anglè
beg v. mòyzava, mangàv, prosizavà
begging n. màngiba
begin v. astàr (e), astaràv (s)
begin! imp. astàr!
behavior n. ìkeriba
behind adj. boolyàkoro
behind adv. palàl, pal, paladàn
behind n. bool
believe v. patyàv, apakyàv, patsyàva, apatyàv

bell n. hlòpka
bellows n. mehùy, mihàni, pishòt
belly n. ozì, kootsìk koorkoo, porh (srb)
belly dance n. gyoobètsi
belongings n. shèhya
belt n. kaìsi, koostìk, kolùy
bend down v. harnyovàv
bend v. telyovàv, bangyaràv, bandzyàva
bent adj. bangè, bangyardò
bespattered adj. cshoongadimè
best man n. kirvòo, kirvò
bet n. marazà, marazàs,
bet v. keràva marazas
beyond adv. kolè [in the other world,
      i.e. beyond "o kolè dyoonyaste"]
big adj. barò, baròo
billy goat n. boozò
birch n. brezà
bird n. chiriklò
bliss n. bakh, bah
bitch n. jooklì
bite n. bòoka, dàndeliba
bite v. hav, dandàv, dandelàv
bitten adj. dandeldò
bitter adj. kerkò
black adj. kalòo, kalò
black magic n. bibahtali (srb)
black olive n. maslìnka
black pepper n. kalòo pipèri

Black Sara n. Bibiyaka (srb) (i.e. May Day
    goddess)
Black Sea p. n. Kalò Deryàv
blacksmith n. boorgoojìs
blacksmith's hearth n. vìnga
blacksmith's spot n. rastìri
blacksmiths n. lohar, the name of the
    "blacksmiths" Gypsy tribe
blanket n. odeàlos
blind adj. korlòo, kovròo, korò,
    bi-akhàkero
blindness n. koripè
blink v. marsa tu yakha [lit. "I strike
    my eyes"] (s)
bloat v. pookeràv
blood n. rat (srb)
bloody adj. ratvalyaràv, ratvalilò, ratvalò
bloom v. looloogyovàv
blotch n. pùpka
blow n. chàlaiba
blow v. phoodàv, chalaybì
blow! imp. phòode!
blue adj. siyòo
blush v. lolyaràv
board n. kanzì, sanzì
board v. inkyàva
boast v. asharàs
boat n. lòdka
body n. mas, tyàlos, snàga

143

boil n. pooknì, phookni,
boil over n. vràsi
boil v. keravav, karavàv, tashtìnav
bolt n. vint
bone n. kòkalos, kokalòos, kokalò
boneless adj. bi-kokalàngero, mezdrimè
book n. lel, lil
boot n. bootòoshi
bootlicker n. mindjomòoyos [lit. "one who licks vaginas"]
booze (sl) v. chalàstra (sl) [from "strike one;" see chalàv = strike]
border n. bàra
bore v. cshingeràva
borrow v. oojilè
bosom n. brekh
Bosphoros p.n. Poravdì [lit. "The crack"]
boss n. manòok
bottle n. shishè, shedès
bottom n. dìbi
bottom parts, genitals n. bool [lit. my husband is tupping me "del man boole mo rom"]
bow (of a violin) n. kharlòo, harlò
bowel n. port
bowl n. charò
bow-string n. tetivà
boy n. chavò, cshavò

braid n. choorì, godì, gozì [to take your brain i.e surprise "telya ti gozi"]

bran n. shùya, shelyà

branch n. dàli, salchìn

branchy adj. salchinyalò

brandy n. pàrniya, pàrnopis, tharì

bread n. marò, maròo, abè (sl)

bread-trough n. balanì

break down v. phagàva

break to pieces v. pegeràv, hoorgyaràv

break v. phagàv, paryovàv, v.

breast n. kolìn, koolìn

breathe v. mozì

bribe n. talàl vastès

brick n. tòohla, kirpìy

bride n. borì

bridge n. proot

bridle n. kantarmas

bring out v. ikalàv

bring here! imp. an ahtè!

bring out! imp. ikàl!

bring v. anàv, antàva

bring! imp. anta!

bristle n. vrutsa

broom n. shoovàl

brother n. phral

brother-in-law n. jès, zhush, salò

brotherly adj. pralikanò

brought n. andì
brunette adj. kaleshrèskoro
build v. keràva
built adj. kerdì
Bulgaria p.n. Dasikanipè
Bulgarian adj. dasikanès, dasikanò
Bulgarian n. das
bull n. bikos, bikoos, bohos
bum n. pirootnò
bundle n. demèti, demètsi
burial n. parhoodìlis
buried adj. pathoomyà, parhoomì
burn n. tablyàv, thabatyàv, thabila, thablyovàv
burned out n. thablyòl
burn v. thabaryàv v.
burning plamniselo
bury v. paronàv
bush n. shrubbery
business deal n. ahàyas
but conj. amà
butcher v. cshinàv
butter n. khil
butterfly n. peperòoga
buttock n. hùlbookoos
button hole n. khuv
button n. kochàk
buy v. tsinàva, kinàv, kinovàv
buy! imp. zhatsin!

C

cab n. faytòy

cabbage n. shah

cage n. kòometsi

calf n. mooskàri

call! imp. chendilis! (s)

call v. revizava (s)

can v. ashti, aschì [I can do that "ashchi keràv adavkà"], shày

can't naschì, nashtì

candle n. memeli, momeli, momì

cane n. rlan, bastòoy, bastoy, rluy

canine adj. rikonanò

cap n. kepe, stadìlk

captured adj. palnò

card n. lel

card v. brivàv (e), brivava (s)

careless adj. moohanàti

carob (bot) n. shoongoori

carpenter n. dooramajìs, oostàs kashèskoro, dooramazhìs

caress v. galì zavàlis

carrot n. morkoos (s)

carry across v. nakhovàv

carry n. igelàv

carry out v. ikilàv

carry v. ingàv, keràva

cart driver n. arabajìs

cart n. vurdò, voordò, talìga, vurdon (pers)

carving knife n. choori

cat n. pisìka, tsitsey, tsitsày, tsitsùy, màchka

cat's adj. tsitsayàkoro

catch a cold v. shoodryovàv

catch up with v. terasùslis, resàv

catch up with! imp. res!

cattle n. pl. gooriya f., gooroova m. (s)

caught adj. astardò

cauldron n. kakavì, haranìya

ceiling n. tavànoos

cellar n. mazès, izbà

center n. mashkàr

century n. shul bresh

ceramic pot n. pirì

chain n. sinjiri, bookagìes

chair n. skomi, skami, skomyànoos

change n. smenìdas

charcoal n. oomblal

charm v. baynàv

chase out v. ipalàv

cheap adj. ooshitsi

cheek n. cham, csham

cheese n. kìral, tsiràl

cheese pie n. miriklì, milìna

cherry n. kiretsì

chest n. gyoosì

chew v. chami-keràv, chamkèrav

chew! imp. chemkerèl!
chewed up adj. chamkerdò
chicken adj. chavryakò
chicken n. havrì, cshavrì
chief adj. sheroonò
child n. chàvo, cshavò, kuzùy
child adj. chavorkanò
childhood n. tsiknipè
childish adj. chavikanò
childless adj. bi-chavèngero, halòo
chill n. marhostì,
chill v. shoodryalyàv
chin n. chenès
choke v. tagavàv
choke, drown v. taslyivàv
chop! imp. tsèpezi!
christen v. boldò
christian adj. krustimè
christening n. ayòs.
Christmas n. Sivrikes, Kolàda, Bozhìk
church adj. khangeryàko, kangeryàko
church n. khàngerì, kangerì
cigarette n. tsigara
cinema n. kinos
circle v. tooryànav
circled adj. panilò
circling around adv. tooryalìste
circumference n. holtà

circumstances n. ooboohotsyà
circus actor n. tsirkajìs
circus n. tsìrka
citizen n. dizootnò
city adj. dizootnò
city n. fòros, dis, diz, zis
clan n. zhìns
clarinet n. toot, gurnèta
clasp n. tokàs
clay n. chik
clay pitcher n. akooròo
clean adj. shoozhò, oozo
clean v. hoozharàv, shoozharàv, choozharàva,
    soolavàv, khasàva,
cleanliness n. khasà, shoozhipè
climb up n. ikestàv
climb v. inkyàva naprù, inkyàva noprù
climbed up adj. ikestilò
cloak n. chòha
clock n. sahàtsi, sahàti
clogs n. nanalyà, laluè
close adj. pashù
close friend n. pashàl
close v. oochsharàv
closed adj. oochshardò
cloth n. platòos, pohtàn
clothes n. shèhya
clothing n. ooryavzì

cloud n. boolòti, oblatsì

clown n. tsirkajìs

club n. asìya, rovlì

coal burner n. mangui

coal n. angàr

coat v. makhàv

cobbler n. koondoorjìs

coffee maker n. tatòjiya (sl)

coffee n. kafàva, kafe, tàto (sl) [lit. "a hot one"]

coffin n. mohtò, moolikanò, sandùtsi

coin n. parà,

coins n. sastrakàne parès

cold n. shil

cold adj. marhomè, shoodròo, shoodrò

cold n. shoodri

color n. tsvyàtoos

color pattern n. chel

color v. chelava

comb n. kanglì, kangì

comb v. oohlyàv, oohlyavàv

comb! imp. oohlyàv!

combed adj. oohlyavdò

come v. avàv, imp. come! av!

complain v. ravàv man

complaining adj. rovìlapis

complete v. resavàv

conceal v. oocsharàv

conditions n. oobootsyà

constipation n. zàpekoos

cook v. kata-habi [lit. "I'll fix food"]

cook food v. habì keràva [lit. "make food)

copper adj. harkomàtar

copper baking pan n. lengèri

copper bowl n. tàsos

copper caldon n. harkòma, kakui

copper kettle n. hlèmeka

coppersmiths tribe n. pavàzes

copulation n. pireybi

cord n. gaytani

corn n. misìri

corner n. kyoshès, keshès

cornet n. fligòrna, toot

corpse n. lèshi

cough n. has

cough v. hasàv

council of five n. panchayat

count n. gen, gèniba

count v. genàv v.

cousin n. bibe-korò, bratovchèdoos m.,
    bratovchèdka f.

cousin on the aunt side n. tetkàkoro

cover n. kapàtsi, hip

cover v. oostelizava, oocsharàv, oocharàva

covered adj. oocshardò

covered wagon n. tsàra

cow n. gooroovnì

cowardly adv. daranòok
cracked adj. pataselòo
cradle n. kookoozì, kòona
craft n. zanaèthi, zanayàthi
craftiness n. phimipe
craftsman n. oostàs, màstooroos
crafty adj. màstoras, màstooroos
crazy adj. dilò, dilinò
credit n. mahàl
cripple n. bangòo mànoosh
crippled adj. sakatì
crocus n. minzoohàri
crooked adj. pingò (sl)
crooked adj. bangèste, bangyà
crooked legged adj. bangò-pero
cross n. krustos, trooshò
crow n. kalò
crow v. bashàv
crude n. yalò
crumble v. oochikeràv
crust n. kòra
cry n. ròiba
cry v. rovàv, rovàva
cry! imp. rov!
cup n. tahtùy
cupboard n. dolàp, dolapi
curdle v. ooshlyaràv
curdled adj. ooshlò

cured adj. saskyardò
curls n. bookli
current [of a river] n. techènie
curse n. sovèl, àkooshiba
curse v. akooshàva, hahavàv
curse! imp. hahav! akòosh!
curtain n. perdès
custom n. adètsi, adèti
cut off v. cshinavàv
cut off! imp. cshinàv!
cut up v. cshingeràv
cut up! imp. cshingèr!
cut v. cshinàv, cshinàva
cutler n. nozhari
cymbal n. tsimbàli

D
dad (sl) n. dat
dad's adj. dadèskoro
dagger n. kamàs
dance n. khèliba
dance v. khelàva, khelàv
dance! imp. khel!
Danube p.n. Tòona
dare v. tromàv
dark adj. kalò, skootsìzi, karanlùki
darken v. kalyòvav

darkness n. kalipè
dash v. hloinàv
daughter-in-law n. borì
daughter n. cshay, cshaey (srb)
dawn n. givesàlo, yavèn, yavinàti
day n. tsìroos, zes, dives, diès, dis
daytime n. givesè, zivisù, disootnò
dead man n.moolò
dead skin n. mel
deaf adj. kashookòo, kashookò
deal n. arlì
death n. moort (sl)
death n. meribè, mèriba
debtor adj. borchlìs
debtor n. oozhledinò
deep adj. hor, har
deer n. surnà
defeat v. paravàv
defecated adj. hendò
deflowered adj. cshingeryàsla
deformed adj. cshingeryàsla
delay v. mainàv
delaying n.màiba
dell n. har
depth n. horipè
descend v. oohlyàv
descend! imp. oohlyàv!
deserted adj. mooklò, yahvalò

deservedly adj. mahàl
destruction n. ejèli
devil n. beng
devil's adj. bengikanò
diaper n. fàskya
diaphragm [anat] n. madès
diarrhea n. diyàriya, syòorgyòoy
dice n. zar
die v. meràv, meràva
dig v. cshapava, hràndav, hràndav, handàv
dig! imp. ravìn!
diligently adj. boolsyarnòo
diminish v. tsinkyovàv
dingy adj. chadimè
dip in water v. boldò
dirt n. melalipè n.
dirty adj. melalò, joongalò
disappear! imp. le te yakhà!
dish n. charò, cinìya
distaff n. hòorka
distance n. dooripè
ditch n. vàda
do not understand v. na-ahàyava
doctor n. saskyarno, drabalò
doe-rabbit n. shoshnì
doesn't listen v. nakandàva
doesn't want v. namangàva
dog n. rikonò, jookèl, zhookél

dog adj. zhooklanòo, rikanoonò, zhooklanò
doggie n. jooklè
doll n. kòokla
domestic adj. kerèskoro
don't v. sharàs
donkey adj. heranò
donkey n. hur, khur
door n. dar, oodàr, voodàr
double-dealer n. dooymooyalò
dough n. homèr, hoomèr
doughy adj. hoomeralò
doughlike adj. hoomerèstar
dove n. gùluba, goorgoorìtsa
down adv. telì, telè, talòl
doze v. lindràv
draft n. techènie
drag v. iglàv
dragon n. lamyà
drawers n. telonì soste, teyunì sostè
dream n. bezèti, soonò
dream v. soonòdikhav, sunòoyzava,
dregs n. tevlès
dress n. òoritoot, fustàni, ooryàv, pogyà
dress up refl. doozdìnavman
dress up v. doozdìnav, podènav
dress! imp. oorìtoot!
dressed adj. ooryavdò
drill n. boorgòo, boorgìya

drill v. khevliryàv, hevlyàrav

drink v. chalàstra (sl) [from "strike one"]

drink v. piav, kàpis, pyàva, matòo, piìs, piyàv

drink one's fill v. makyovàv

drip v. choolyàl , choolyanav, tavdalàv

dripping n. tavdanilò

drive in v. dengyaràv

drive v. tràdav

drop n. choolì

drought n. shookipè

drowned adj. tasavdò

drum n. daòoli, davùli, bang

drumstick n. ròoy

drunk adj. màtis, matò

drunkenness n. matibè

dry adj. shookò

dry out v. shookyovàv

dry v. shookyaràv

dumb adj. rarorò

dung n. goshnyà

duplicity n. dooimooyalipè

during the day adv. diesè

during the night adv. rat

dusk n. parla, parila

dust n. pràhos

dusty adj. csharyalò, phoordoo

duties n. oojlipè n.

E

ear n. kan
early adj. yavìn
earring n. chenì, cshun, chun, chuy
earthen jug n. khorò, akhooròo, akooròo
earthen pitcher n. korì
earthquake n. phoov khelèl
Easter n. Pashalì
eat v. hav
eat! imp. ha!
eavesdrop v. dàvkan
Edirne p.n. Durnopoli
educated adj. siklò
egg n. alrò, arò
eggplant n. patlazhùy
egotist n. vìholas, hunzùri
eight n. ohtò, oktò
eight hundred n. ohtòshel
eighteen n. deshohtò
eighty n. ohtòvardesh
elbow n. moogì, khùy, kooy, khooy
elephant n. fìlos
elevated adj. vazdimè
eleven n. deshyèk
embers n. hoy
embrace v. an gùy dyàva
emptied adj. choochardò

emptiness n. choochipè
empty adj. choochò, choochì
empty v. chocharàv, choocharàv
end n. agor
enemy n. dooshmàn
enjoy v. dehàv
enough epesèl
enter v. del
envelopment n. tsipa
epileptic n. bengalò
escape v. htavàv
even adv. varènjak
evening n. rat, iràt
evening time adv. rakyàsa
event n. sloochisàlo
every adj. sèko
evil n. kanilipè
ewe n. bakrì
exactly so kide, ha kide (s)
exhaust oneself v. vrahnyànav
exit v. iklyòvav
expect v. ajaràv
expensive adj. kuchì, pahajìs
eye n. yakh
eyebrow n. phovà
eyeglasses n. gyozlikyà
eyelashes n. tsamtsàlya
eyelids n. klepachì

F

face n. mooy
factory n. hàvrika
fairy tale n. paramise
faith n. àpakyaba
fake adj. hohavnò
falcon n. atmazhàs
fall ill v. naboryànav
fall v. dav, perav, choràv
family tree n. vitsa
famous adj. shoondò
far adv. dooràl
far away adj. door
farmer n. phoovyalò
farrier n. chilingìr
farted adj. kaynyargyas
fast adj. sìgo, sigòo
fat adj. khoyhalò, shoovlò
fate n. oorme (srb)
father n. dad, babà (rare)
father-in-law n. sastrò, sastròo
fatness n. thoolipè
favor n. yardàn
fear v. daràv, dar
feather n. por, peri
February n. tsiknò màsek
feeble adj. kishlò
feebly adj. slàbo

feed v. parvaràv, parvaràva
feel ashamed v. lajàv
female pigeon n. goorgoorìtsa
feminine adj. joovlikanò
femininity n. joovlipè
fence n. zagradimè, bar
field adj. oomalyàko
field n. avlìn, kuri, oomàl
fifteen n. deshoopànch
fifth adj. panshtò
fifty n. peìnda, penìda
fifty thousand n. peìnda milyà
fig n. cshàmika, chamikà
fig tree n. nachimikìn
fight n. maribè, asharibè
figure out v. dikhàv
file n. pilà, yar, rini
file v. rininàv
filed adj. rinimè
filled up adj. phooklò
find v. arakhàv [find the road "arakhav o drom"]
finger n. nay, angooshtò, angoostò, angooshtòo
fingernail n. nay, nayà
fire n. yak
firelog n. kash
fireplace n. ojàkoos, tsedèl, rastsirì
first adj. avgò, èkto
fish adj. machèsko

fish n. macshò
fish bone n. macshèskoro karò
fisherman n. machàri
fishy adj. macshanò
fist n. doomookh, doomòok
five n. panch
five hundred n. pàncshel
flag n. bayratsi
flame n. flòga
flat stone n. lamàda
flea n. pooshoom, pishoom
fleecy rug n. tsurhà
fleshy adj. masalò
flint and iron n. chakmàkoos, chakmàk
flint and steel n. amnaryòo
floor n. deshemès
flour n. arò, aròo
flow v. athavdav, thàvdav
flower n. looloodì
flute n. flèyta
fly n. makhì
fly v. ooryàv
fog n. mòohli
fold v. kapladìnav
follow v. dendìnav
food n. hamoos, khamoos, habè [something to
      eat "hab-naske"]
fool n. ahmàki, chalkìya, balamò (sl)

foolish adj. chalalì
foolish man n. ahmàtsi manoosh
for you tookè
forehead n. chikat, chekàt, chokàt
foreign adj. avèr
foreigner n. gajòo, gajò
"foreigners" tribe n. gorbati
forest adj. veshootnò,veshinò
forest n. besh, vesh, vosh (pers)
forester n. veshtahàr
foretell v. prehoratinàv
foreward adv. naanglè
forge n. rastìri
forget v. bisteràv, bistràva
fork n. pantaròolya, banèla, bonèla
forteen n. deshooshtàr
forty n. sarànda
forty thousand n. saranda milyà
fountain n. cheshmyà
four n. shtar
four hundred n. shtàrshel
fox n. lisitsa
freeze v. paoosàv, marhònav
Friday n. pharastsivì, paraskoovìn, parastsivi
friend [from the same gang] n. avèr (sl)
friend n. pral, amàl
friends n. hanamika (srb)

friendship n. amalipè
frog n. zhàmba, panyalì, jàmba
from prep. andarò, andàr, kàthar
from the inside adv. andràl
from there adv. othàr, okòthar
from where adv. kàtar
front one adj. angloonò
frost n. pàhni
frozen adj. pahomè
fruit n. emishi
frying pan n. tsihàni
full adj. phèrdo, cshalù, chalyardò
full of money adj. hatalì
fur hat n. kalpàtsi
furness n. bof

G
gain weight v. pheryàva, thoolyovàv
gall n. holì
gallbladder n. fèra
gambler n. marazajìs
garbage n. shtòopos
gardener n. bahchovanjìs
garlic n. sir
gate n. dar
gather v. khidàva , kizyàva, kidav

gathered adj. khizim
gay adj. koyorvalo
gem n. kòochibar
get! imp. lav
get cured v. saskyovàv
get drunk v. matyovàv
get fat v. khoynàlyovav
get involved v. ehminàv man
get mad v. holihàv
get scared v. trashanàv
get tired v. khinìlyovav, kinisyàv
get up v. oohtyàv
Get up! imp. oohti!
get v. astràv
ghastly adj. moolikanò
gift n. armagànos
girdle n. gerdèy
girl n. chay, cshay
give! imp. kay!
give v. dav, dyàva
give a bath v. nanyaràv
give v. del
give! imp. kay! [give me "kay mande"]
give! imp. an! [give it to me! "mande an!"]
give birth v. bianàv
glass cup n. tahtày
glass n. jàmi, zhemì, tsuklòs
gloves n. pl. vastèskeri

gnaw n. choopinàv
go v. jav, dav
go around v. trooyanyàv
go crazy v. delinovàv
go! imp. ja!
goat meat n. boozì ekomas
goat n. f. booznì, boozì
goat n. m. boozò
God n. devèl, del
godfather n. boldò
gold n. sovnà
golden adj. sovnalò
golden coins n. frolì, gàlbeya
golden neckless n. muna
golden ring n. somnakày
goldpanners n. auràri
gone adj. gelè
good adj. shookàr, lacshò
good adv. lacshès
good evening! voc. lacshì ti rat
good mood n. kef
good morning! voc. lachshì tì yavìn!, bahtalì ti
    avin!
good night! voc. lokì ti rat
goodbye! voc. jidikhibnàs!, achshòv devlèsa!
goods n. stòka
goose n. papìn
gorge n. boàzi

graft v. hashlàva
grain n. zhov
grandaughter n. cshavesko cshei (srb),
    cshavesko cshay
grandfather n. papòo
grandfather n. papo (srb), papòos
grandmother n. mami (srb)
grandson n. cshavesko cshav
grape adj. drakhèngeri
grape juice n. mùstenitsa
grapes n. drak, drakhà, drakh
grass n. char
grave n. mòri, mìmoras
gravestone n. bar morìskoo
gravel n. chahkùy, chakùl
gravel worker n. chakuzhìs
graveyard n. mìmorya, limòri, mimòri
graze v. charavàv, charàv
graze! imp. charàv!
greasy adj. maznoo, khilyardò
great thing n. baripè
Greece p.n. Elàda
greedy adj. kurlalò
Greek n. balamò
Greeks n. pl. elìnya
green adj. yeshìl, zelèno, charyalò
greet v. resàv
grey adj. suy

grill n. skàra
grime n. mel
groan n. hondibà
groan! imp. hòndin!
ground meat n. chentimè
ground n. phoov
grow dark v. rakyòvav
grow dumb v. raròlyovav
grow dumb! imp. ràrolyov!
grow old v. pooranyàv
grow v. baryovàv
gruel n. mianès
grumpy adj. hoynalòo
guess! imp poonjari!
guilt n. dosh n.
guitar n. chalkìya, kitàra
gun n. pistolètoos
gunpowder n. barutsì
gush v. hloìn
guts n. porlyà
gutter n. gerdèy
Gypsy adj. romanò
Gypsy blacksmiths n. pl. boorgoojìdes
Gypsy Bulgarian n. jorò
Gypsy camp style adj. tsarunò
Gypsy camp tent n. tsàra
Gypsy horse traders n. lovàrya
Gypsy husband n. rom

Gypsy n. rom
Gypsy spindel-makers n. vlahyà
Gypsy style music n. chàlga
Gypsy tinker n. pavàzya
Gypsy tradition n. romanipè
Gypsy way n. romanipè
Gypsy wife n. romnì
Gypsy woman n. romnì

H
haggard adj. kishlò
hail n. kookoodì
hair lock n. bal
hair n. balà
hair pin n. foorkèti, fìba
hairy adj. balalò
half n. ekvàsh, epkàsh
halter n. shoovàr
halvah n. halvàs, halvà
hamburger n. kyooftès
hamlet n. gavorò
hammer n. chookòos, chikìs, sivrì
hammer v. chookìzava
hand n. vas, vast
hand over v. podày zavà, dodàv, doodàv
hand over! imp. ashtà!
handcuffs n. bookagìes
handfull n. boornèk

handle n. destò, drùzhka

hang v. oomblavàv

happening n. sloochisàlo

happiness n. baht (srb), loshanipè, loshalì, bakh, bah

happy adj. loshalò, batalo (srb), loshanò, bahtalò

hard salami n. cshoozhòokoos, soojookoos

harden v. zoràlyovav

haste n. sìgyariba

hat n. stadì, sasti

hatch v. bianàv

hate v. mrazìzava

haul v. tsìdav

have v. isì

hay n. khas, kas

hazelnut n. pendèh

he pron. odà, onà

head n. shòro, sherò

headache n. sharoo dookhala

heal v. sastaryàv, saskyarav

health n. sastipè

healthy adj. sastò, vestò, zoralò

hear v. shoonàv

heart n. ilò, ilòo, ozì

hearth n. ojàkoos, komna

heat up v. tataryàv

heaven n. del

heavenly adj. devletlùki

heavy adj. parò, pharòo

hedgehog n. kanzavurì, taralèzhoos

heel n. patòon, khoor, payòom

height n. oochipè

heir n. mirahchìs

held adj. doldò

hell n. jandò, jendèmi

help n. yardàn

help v. akandàv

hemp n. oosh

hen adj. kahnyàkoro

hen n. kafì, kahnì

her pron. la

herd n. chàrda

herd v. charàv

herder n. gopt

"herders" tribe n. goptyà

here adv. athè, akì, kutkà, àke

hero n. moorsh

heroism n. moorshibè

hers pron. làkoo, perì

Hey, maiden! voc. cshae!

Hey, you! voc. cshavàlen!

hiccup n. hlùchkoba

hiccup v. hultsìzava, hluchkònav

hidden adj. garavdò

hide v. garavàv, garavamàn, garàv man

172

high adj. oochòo, oochò
highway n. shosès
him pron. les, lis
hinge n. minteshès
hire v. yavàlis butsèti
his pron. liskòo, lèskoro
hit the mark v. tsezelyaslis oocshoroo
hit v. chalàv
hit! imp. lama!
hit! imp. chalàv!
hoe n. bèteltsa, mudìka
hold v. ikeràv, astràv
hold! imp. ikèr!
hole n. huv, hev, khuv
hole in the ground n. har
holiday n. patragì (vlh)
holy adj. choochò
home adj. kherootnò
home n. dòmos
honesty n. pitav
honey n. avgìn
honor n. gyoosì
hoof n. khoori (s)
hook n. kooka
hoop n. hem, kololòos
hope n. òozdiba,
hope v. nadìv, oozdinàv man
horizon n. devlèskere pògya

horn n. shing
horse adj. grastani
horse n. gras
horse race n. kooshìya
horse trader n. grastèngoro
horse traders n. zhambazi
horse-gear n. tukumyè
horse-shoe n. petaloos, pètalos, vòoda
horseshoe nail n. karfì
hospital n. dookhanì
hot taste adj. tharòo, taròo
hot adj. tatòo
hour n. sahàti, sahàtsi
house n. kher
housemaid n. halaìnka
how adv. sar, sap
how are you? sar sinyàn?
how many? kitì?
how much? kibòr, kibir [how much does it cost? "kibir kerla?"]
human adj. manooshkanò
humid adj. nemlìs
humiliate oneself v. moostàchi
hunchback n. bangòo mànoosh
hunger n. bakhalòosi, bokh
hungry adj. bokhalò
hurriedly adv. sigyarindòs
hurry v. sigyaràv

hurts v. dookhàl man
husband n. rom
hyacinth n. zyoombyòol
hypocrit n. doomooyalò

I
I pron. me
ice n. pahòs
icicles n. pl. choochooryà
if conj. te
ill adj. naboryamè, nasvalò
illness n. nasvalipè, naboryàsti
image n. òmnyazos
immortal adj. bi-milò
in ki
in prep. ko
in front adv. ahglàl, chekatèste
in the middle adv. mashkaràl
in vain adv. tevekeliès adv.
industrious adj. bootsyarnoo
infidelity n. inkyàri
inflate v. pookeràv
injustice n. bangipè
inn keeper n. mehanjìs
innards n. bookò
inside adv. andrè, andì
instead so
insufficient adj. kùti

insulted adj. holankyargyàs
intestines n. andronibè
into adì
intoxicate v. makyaràv
intoxicated adj. makyardò
intoxication n. màkyariba
invite v. kanìzava
iron adj. srastoonò
iron n. sàstra, sras, srast, srastrakàni
ironsmith n. tamar
"ironsmiths" tribe n. boorgoojìdes
irresponsible adj. bi-godyàtyero
is si
isn't it so? di?
Israel p.n. Jootanipè
Istanbul p.n. Polinà
it hurts v. dookal
itch n. ger, handjòl, soozàv
it's all the same to me me-karèste
    vulg. (sl)
ivory n. fildishi

J
jack ass n. her
jagged adj. dandalò
jam v. tuktinav
January n. barò màsek

jaws n. chamàhoolya
jay n. kakaràshka
jenny-ass n. hernì
Jew n. joot, chifòotsi, chifòot
Jewish adj. jootanò
jingle v. drunkìzava
joint n. kentra
joy n. losh
jump v. hurpìnav
jumping n. hùrpiba
justice n. kris (srb)

K
keep v. arakhàv
kerchief n. dikhlò
key n. klìchoos
kick (with hind legs) n. zuntyà
kick n. lahtì, lahtìdav
kill v. mar (srb), moodaràv
kill! imp. moodàr!
killed adj. moodarè
kind adj. hakikàti
kindhearted adj. hakikàti
kindle v. phabaràv
kindness n. manooshibè
king n. thagàr
kingdom n. thagaripè
kinship n. endanipè

kinsman n. hemanìk
kiss n. choomidinì
kiss v. choomidàv
kissed adj. choomidimè
kissing n. chòomidiba
kitchen n. mootvàki
kitten n. tsikurì
knead v. oochanàv, ooshenàv
kneaded adj. ooshendò
kneading n. òosheniba
kneading-trough n. skafidì
knee n. koch, kocsh
knife n. cshoorì, chorì, cshorì
knit v. khoovàv, koovàv, khoovàva
knitting n. khòoviba
knock v. maràv
knot n. koch, kòmbos
know v. poongaràva, pinjaràv, zhanava, janàv
knowledge n. boojandò
knowledgeable adj. boojandò

L
lace n. gaytani
ladder n. stùlba
lake n. èzeri, èzeroos
lamb adj. bakranò
lamb meat n. bakranò
lamb n. bakrò

lame adj. bangò, sakatì

lamp n. lamba

land n. tan, phoov

language n. chib

lard n. khonì, koni'

large adj. barò

largest adj. hem barò

last adj. agorunò

last night adv. iblòl

last year adv. pèrsi

late adv. gechi

later adv. jinèhari

laugh n. àsaba

laugh v. asàv

laugh! imp. asà!

laughter n. àsaba

lay (eggs) n. mutìzila

lazy adj. marzàl

lazybones n. marzanòok

lead v. ingàv

leaf n. patrìn

leak v. tavdalav

lean adj. shookò

lean against v. podpirisalma, propinàv

learned n. sikavdò

learning n. sìkliba

leather n. tabàk, kozhà, morthì

leather shop n. tabàhna

leave v. mookàv, achàv
leave! imp. mook!
lead v. koorshooy
lee n. oolòov, zavet
left adj. ozhoovyanò, joovèl rig
left side n. zhoovèl rig
leftovers n. bàberka
leg n. changò, chang
lemonade n. limonàda
length n. loongipè
lentil adj. lintàkeri
lentils n. lìnta
let v. nek, ne
let's go! imp. haydi!
letter n. lil, lel
lick v. charàv
lick! imp. char!
licy adj. zhoovalòo
lid n. hip
lie n. hohayba, hohaybè,
lie v. hohavàv
lie! imp. hohàv!
lift v. vàzdav
light adj. lokò
light n. tsìbriba
light up v. tharav
lightning n. svetkavitsa
lightning strikes sevinel

like prep. sap
like v. doovàv
lime n. kirèch, kirechi
line n. cherta, lìniya
lion adj. sinhanò
lion n. sinhày, aslàni, lùvos
lioness n. sinhanì
lip n. oosh, voosh
lipstick n. lolipè
listen v. kandàva
listen! imp. shoon!
lively adj. shìnilis
liver n. bookò, kalinjò, yooloo, yoolroo
living n. jìviba
lizard n. shapòorka
load n. paripè
load v. ladavàv, làdaiba
loaded adj. ladavdò
loading n. làdaiba
loathe v. joongàv v.
local adj. thanootnò, atharootnò
lock v. pandàv
lock n. klyòochalka
locked adj. panlò
log n. moolooklì
long adj. loongo
long ago adv. chiràla
look like v. prepàv

look v. dikhàv
loom n. stanoos
lordly adj. hoolanyàkoro
lose v. nashalàv
lose weight v. kishlyolàv, arazhyava
loss n. zyan, zaràri
lost adj. nashaldòo
louse n. joov, zhoo
lousy adj. joovalò, zhoovaloo
love each other mangèn pes
love n. dèhiba, pireylapis
love v. kamav, dèhav
lover n. piryamlòo
low adj. teloonò,
low adv. harnèste
low round table n. yàstagachi
lowland n. harnipè
luck n. kusmèti, kusmètsi
lunch n. obyadòoski
lunchtime n. obyadòoski

M
Macedonian Gypsies n. gyooptès
mad adj. delinò
madness n. delinipè
magic n. drab
magician n. dèvi
maiden n. cshay

make sounds v. bashàv
make! imp. ker!
mallet n. baròo chookòos
man n. moorsh, manòosh
manliness n. moorshibe
March n. martakoo
mare n. grasnì
market n. koorkò
market place n. zis
married adj. prandemè
marry v. piltsèyla
marsh n. azmàtsi
master n. hoolanò
matches n. kibrìti
matchmaker n. henamìka
mayor n. cheribashì
me pron. man
measles n. cshèl
measure n. haràri
measure against v. marazàs
measured adj. tsidimè
meat n. mas
medicine n. drab
medlar n. mòoshmin
medow n. chayri
meeting n. kìdiba
membrane n. tsìpa
men's adj. moorshikanès

mend v. kurpìzavà
mention v. andìnav
merchandise n. malì, stòka
merchant v. toojàri
mercury n. zhivàkos
middle n. mashkarò
midnight n. mashkari rat
mildew n. mòohli
milk adj. thoodvalò
milk n. thoot , toot
milk v. doshàv, dooshàv
mill-stream n. len, vàda
miller n. asiavjìs, asvayèngoro, dermenzhìs
millet n. koormì, khoormì
mimicking adv. rarorikanès
mince v. chentinàv
mind n. gozì
mindless adj. bi-godyàtyero
mine pron. mi, mo, morlòo
minute n. minòota
miracle n. nàmi
mirror n. aynàs
miser n. stiptsàr, pahajìs
miserable adj. rugyalò
misery n. rùgya
mislead v. ooshtinkyàrav
mistake n. dosh
mistress n. hoolanì

mix v. ehminàv
mixed adj. ehmimè
moist adj. soslò
molar n. thar
Moldavia p.n. Moldovà
Monday n. ponedèlnikoos, palalkoorkò
money (sl) n. màngis
money n. lovè, lèvoos, parès, hatalì
money-dealer n. loventsa rom
moneyless adj. bi-parèngero
money-lusting adj. parà-gyozi
monger n. loventsa rom
monkey n. shebètsi
monster n. boholyàchi
month n. màsek, cshon
monthly adv. masekèste
moon n. chon, cshon, màsek, choormoot,
more pànda
morning n. sabàlen, andiyavìn, avìn
morning sickness adj. ashardìnel
mortar n. havànchis, havanchitoos
moslem Bulgarian n. pomàtsi
mosque n. jamiya
most adv. hem
most n. nay
mother n. duy, day, dey (srb)
mother's adj. dayàkoro
mother-in-law n. sasòoy, sasùy

mount v. ooklyovàv
mount a horse v. hepvizava
mountain n. plàyna, vesh
mouse n. germoosò, germoosòo, kermoosò
moustache n. moostàtse
mouth n. mooy
mow v. kosìzava
much noot, boot, haylì
mud n. chik, tevlès
mud v. chikàlyovav
muddy adj. chikalo
mulberry n. dutsìn, dootsìn
mule n. jorò, jòri, katùra
multi-colored adj. koyorvalò, kotoralò
municipal building n. prètoora
murder n. mòodaribe
murdered adj. moodardò
murderer n. moodarò, moodarnò
muscle n. mooskoolis, mooskoola
mushroom n. papòohi,
mushrooms [amanitae] n. hoohoorà
music n. bàshilba, bashalipè
musician n. chalgajìs, bashaldòo,
        bashalnò
must v. trèbinal, mangèlpes
mute adj. lalooroo
mutton n. barkanò
muzzle n. mòosoora, zoorlà

my pron. morlòo
my pron. mi

N
nail n. karfì, eksèri
nail v. chookìzava
naked adj. nangò, oonangi
name n. akanà, alàv [what is your name?
    "sar si to alav?"]
narrowness n. tangipè
narrow v. tangyàrav
narrow adj. tang
naughty adj. levavdò
near adv. pashù, pashè
neck n. men
necklace n. miriklè, gerdèy
needle n. soov, ey, soo
neighborhood n. màhala
nephew n. pralisko cshow
nervousness n. tetìki
net n. mrezhyà
nettles n. tsikìnda
never adv. nìkhana
new adj. nevò
news item n. necipè
nice adj. bootlàchoo, dehoonòok
night n. rat
nighttime ratsyàsa, rakyàsa

nine n. eynà, eyà
nine hundred n. eynàshel
ninety n. eynàvardesh
ninth adj. eyatò
nipple n. porl
nit n. likh
nitty adj. likhalò
no na
none nìsavo [not one kind of a person]
no [do not]! imp. ma!
no one khònik, konìk [no single person]
no way nìsar
noise n. gyoorooltìya
nomad Gypsies n. kardaràsha
non-Gypsy boy n. raklò
non-Gypsy girl n. raklì
non-Gypsy n. gajò
nose n. nak, nakh
nostril n. hùrni
nothing kànchik, khanchìk
now adv. akanà
nurse v. choochì del
nursing mother n. choochvanì

O
oak n. karachì, meshès
oak tree n. mashàva
oath n. sovèl

oats n. jov
obliged adj. oojlò
observation n. dèndiba
obstinacy n. inatsi
occupation n. zanayètsi
occurance n. sloochisàlo
officer n. fitsèri
official n. gomi
offspring n. jornì
ointment n. màkhiba
old adj. phoorano, poorèi, pooranòo
old man n. papòo
old woman n. poorèi roomì
older brother n. moo baròo phral
older sister n. dàda
on foot adv. pesh
on prep. e
on top adv. oopral
once n. èkhvar
once upon a time adv. dekanà
one hundred n. shel
one n. ek, yek, ekh
one o'clock n. ek sahàti
one thousand n. mìlya
onioned adj. siryalò
only adj. sadè, ekipè
opposite adv. mamooèste
orchestra n. orkèstoorus

orphan n. chorò
other adj. avrès
our pron. amaròo, amarò
outrun v. izprevarizehìs
outside adj. avrì
oven n. bov, bof
overflow v. tashtìnav
owl n. boohaloos
ox adj. gooroovèskaro
ox n. gooròov, gooròo

P
padlock n. klyadì
pain n. dook, dookh, dookhàl, paripè
paint n. boyà
paint v. makhàv
pal n. pral (sl)
palace n. palàtos
palm n. boornek
pan n. tavà
pannier n. panèri
pants n. pantolyà
paper adj. lilèstar
paper n. il, ilìnga
paradise n. jenletsi
pass v. nakhàv
pass! imp. nakh!
paste v. maràv

pastrami v. pastarmà
path n. putèka
pavement n. palyà
pay v. pokinàv, platsìzava
pay! imp. platsizì!
peak n. vrùhoos
peanut n. fastutaya
pear n. ambròl
pear tree n. ambrolìn
peasant adj. gavootnò
peasant n. gavèstar
peasant woman n. gavoodnì
peg-top n. furfalak, dzvinka
pen n. perodrùshka
pencil n. molyàvoos
penis n. kar
people n. indais, sinti (srb)
perforate v. hevlyaràv
perforate! imp. hevlyàr!
perforated adj. hevlyardò
perish v. phiràv, piràv
permit v. mookàv
person n. jenò
pestle n. chookàlos
Pharaoh n. firaòoni, firavòni
phoenix n. charani
pick n. bèteltsa
picked adj. bridvà

pie n. pita
piece n. parchès, kotòr
piece together v. ekledìnav
pieced together adj. ekledimè
pierce v. posavàv, hevlyaràv
pig n. baychòo, buychòo
piglet n. balichò
pigskin sandal n. tsaròoy
pigsty n. kòchina
pile n. tsìla
pillow n. sherànd
pimple n. pùpka
pin down! imp. poonjàr!
pin up v. boonzharàv
pine n. bòroos
pipe n. loolàva
piss v. mootràva
pitcher n. khorò
place n. than, tan, diz (pers)
plait n. plìtka, chochopi
plant v. ispelàv
plaster v. makhàv
plate n. charò, chinìya
play (a game) v. khelàva
play (an instrument) v. bashalàva
play cards v. kahàla kartìndi
play music v. bashàla, bashalàv
playing ground n. tanàli

pleasant adj. lacshòo, lacshò
pledge n. armanyà
pleshka n. pikòo
pliers n. kerpedèy
plough v. ravinàv
plough! imp. rivìn!
ploughing n. hràndina
pluck v. kooshàv
plucked adj. brivdà
plum adj. khilyavinìngeri
plum n. kilyavìn, khilyavìn, erikin, tooyavìn
plum brandy n. khilyavinèngeri thari
plum tree n. khilyavin, tsiyava
plume n. bal, por
pocket knife n. chekìya
pocket n. jèpa
point out n. sikavàv
poison n. kotlyamè [oxydized copper],
    tsitsèli
poison v. tsitselìnav
poisoning n. tsìtseliba n.
poke n. hràndina
pole n. kilò
police station n. cshooryalì
policeman n. chooryalò, cshooryalò
polisher n. pavàzya
pomegranate n. nàrchi
poor adj. chorò, chovròo

popler n. kavàtsi
porch n. haètsi
pork adj. balichkanò, baycshonòo
portion n. hisès
possibility n. ashtipè
postpone v. mookàv
pot maker n. piryakerò, pirìngoro, kaldaresh (trk)
pot n. strakìna, kaldare (srb)
potato n. mùrgili, kòmpiri
potmaker n. kaldarar (srb)
"potmakers" tribe n. kalderàsh
pour out v. cshordò
pour v. cshoràv
poured out adj. cshordò
poverty n. choripè
power n. zor
powerful adj. zoralò
praise v. asharàva, fuyzàva
prank n. bengipè
pregnancy n. khamnipè
pregnant adj. khamnì, kabnì
press down v. plakonàv
press v. pastardinàv
pressed adj. plakomè
pretend v. keràv man
pretty adj. achòo, lacshòo, lacshò
priest n. rashày , shamdàni, rushùy, rushày

priest's wife n. rashhanì
prison n. phàndiba, panliba
prison (sl) n. phandèla
private adj. poomarè
prop [in a tent] n. berànda
prostitute n. libnì
prostitution n. loobipè
proud adj. barikanò
providence n. stròngya
prune n. siya tooyavìn
puke n. ashàshibe
pull v. tsìdav
pulled adj. tsidimè
pulled down adj. oohlyavdò
pulling n. tsìdiba
pumpkin adj. doodoomalò
pumpkin n. doodòom
punch v. chingeràva
punishment n. taksiràti
puppy n. tsikooroo zhookel
pus n. phub, phoom
push over v. peravàv
pussy adj. ikhaloo
put v. tovàv, thovàv
put on v. podènav
puttees n. patavè, patavì

Q

quarrel v. chingàr

quarrelsome adj. joongalò, chingaralo

queen n. thagarnì

quicksilver n. zhivàkos

quiet adj. parus

quilted jacket n. hurkàs

quince n. goodooìn

quirk n. bengipè

R

rabbit adj. shoshoèskoro

rabbit n. shoshòy, shoshùy

racing n. kooshiyèti

rag n. partsùy, korò

railway station n. garà

rain n. brishìnt, brishìm

rain v. brishìm del, del

rainbow n. breshimdalò koostik

raindeer n. karajàs

rainy adj. brishimdalò

raise a hand v. vàzdav vas

ram n. bakrò, bakròo, kòchi

rash n. haspàs

rat n. plùhoos

ravage v. yahvalò

raw adj. sooslò

razor n. oostràs, brusnàchi

reach v. resàv
read v. chetinàv, genàva, genàv
reading n. gèniba
ready adj. hazùri
real adj. chachoonò
really adv. chachestè
reap v. randàv
reaped adj. randimè
rear n. paloonipè
recognize v. penjaràv
red adj. lolòo, lolò
reed n. papòor
reek v. kandàv
regal adj. thagarutnò
rein n. gèmi n.
reject v. nikamàva
rejoice v. loshanàv, loshazyava
relative n. endanì, pashàl
remember v. delpesgodì
remind n. delgodì
repulsive adj. joongàkoro
respect n. sàydiba
respect v. saidìnav
respected adj. saydimè
rest v. noonchìzava
return n. ìriba
return v. irìnav
return! imp. ìrin!

returned adj. irimè

revenge n. hùzi, garèzi

rheumatism n. tsihà

rib n. pashavrò, rèbroos

rice n. arìtsi

rich adj. manginalò, barvalò, barvalòo

ridicule v. aprasàv

rifle n. parordì, pòoshko

right-hand side n. moorsh rig, chachi rig (srb)

right here adv. èke

righteous adj. choochò, chachoonò

ring n. angroostì, angroostsì

rinse v. halavàv

rinsed adj. halavdo

rip v. cshinàv

ripen v. resàv

rise [get up, elevate] v. koohtyàv, badàvaman

rise [increase in volume] v. kabardinàv

rissole n. kebàpchitoos

river adj. leynàkaro

river n. len

river-bank n. bryàgoos

road n. drom

roast v. pekàva

roasted adj. peklò

rob v. choràv

robbery n. choribè

rock n. barà

roll v. valyànav
rolled adj. valyamè
roof n. oocharibè
rooster n. bashnò, bashnòo
rope n. shelò
rotten adj. kermò
rub n. mòriba
rub v. moràv
rub! imp. mor!
rubbed adj. mordò
rug n. patò, tsèrha
rump n. kùchi
rumple v. hoomìnav
rumpled adj. hoomimè
run into debt v. oodjlyovàv
run v. prastàv, prastàva, nashàv,
run! imp. nash!
runaway n. nashtò
running n. nàshiba
running away n. nàshiba
rush-mat n. roohoozìna

S
sabre n. sàbya
sack n. gonò, gonoò, haranì, ravalì, ràvalos
sad adj. tùzhno
saddle n. kaltàk, zen

saddlebags n. pl. hebèdes
sadness n. paripè [I am sad "paripè si mànge"]
sale n. bikyanibè
saloon-keeper n. kiaplyarì
salt n. lon
salt v. longyaràv
salted adj. longyardò
salty adj. londò
sand n. poshi, chishùy
sandals n. sanùy
sated adj. chalò
satisfied adj. chalò
satisfy! imp. chalyàr!
saturate v. chalyovàv
Saturday n. sàvatos, savutoo
sauerkraut n. armì
sausage n. goy
save v. koortarinàva
saved adj. oohtavdò
saver n. oohtavnò
savory n. chòobritsa
saw n. trivònos
say n. vàkeriba
say v. pothàva, penàva, vakerava, phenàv
scabbard n. kapìya
scabies n. ger
scale n. terezìa
scare v. daravàv

scary adj. daràke
scissors n. kat, khakh
scold v. chingadàv
scratch v. harloovàva, haravàv
scream v. revizava
sea n. deryàv, dryàv, denis
seat v. beshtì
seated adj. beshtòo
second-hand adj. pooranèste
second-hand dealer n. vehtoshàre
secretely adv. choryàl
sediment n. tevlès
see v. dikhav
seed n. sèmi
seek v. ròdav
sell v. kanashàv, bikyanàv, bikenàv, bikìnava
send v. bichalàv
separate v. oolavàv
separated adj. oolavdè
separation n. òolaiba
Serb n. sùrbi
servant n. hezmikyàri
serve v. cshoràv, akàndav
settled adj. yerdìles
settled down adj. thanootnò
settled Gypsies n. erlìdes
seven n. eftà
seven hundred n. eftàshel

seventeen n. desheftà
seventy n. eftàvardesh
sew v. sivàv
sewing n. sìiba
shaby adj. chadimè
shade n. syànka
shadow n. oochipè
shady adj. senya
shake v. khelèl
shallow n. plìtoo
shame n. lajavò
shamed on you! imp. lajà!
shameless adj. bi-lajalòo
shave v. mòorav
shave! imp. mooràv!
shaved adj. randlò
shaving n. mooraiba
she pron. odiyà, voy, oy, odyà, yoy
she-bear n. richnì
she-donkey n. herni
she-wolf n. roovnì
sheaf n. garbò
sheared adj. mooravdè
sheep n. bakròo
sheet n. charshàfi
shelter n. oolòov, zavet
shepherd n. charavnò
shine v. pakèl, tsibrìzava

ship n. parahòdoos
shirt n. gad
shit n. koonà, khool
shiver v. lizdràv
shivering adj. lizdravdò
shoe a horse v. petalonàv
shoe n. postey
shoes n. pl. menìse, potinyà, menìya
shoot v. strelìzava
shop n. dyookyàni, dyoogèi
short adj. harnò
short adj. harnò
shorten v. tsinkyaràv, harnyaràv
shotgun n. pooshko, parordi
shoulder n. phikòo, pikò, phikò
shove in v. dengyaràv
shove v. ispelàv
shoved adj. ispeldò
show off v. sharàv
show ones tongue v. angyarèlpes
Shut up! imp. taynè!
shutters n. pl. kepentsyà
shuttle n. sovàlka
shy adj. lajalò
sick adj. nasvalo, nasvalòo
sickle n. loonò, loonòo
side n. rig
sieve n. rèshtos, reshètka

sift v. oocshànav
sifting n. oocshaniba
sigh v. ohkinàv v.
sign n. tabèla
silk adj. keshoonò
silk headkerchief n. purlènta
silk n. kesh, kezh
silver adj. roopoovalò
silver n. roop
sin n. bezèh
sing v. gilyàbav, zàbava, bashàv
singer n. gilyavnò, gilyabnì
singing n. gìlyaiba
sink n. batonava
sister n. phen
sister-in-law n. dòda, zhushtuy
sit v. beshàv
six n. shov
six hundred n. shòvshel
sixteen n. deshooshòv
sixth adj. shovtò
sixty n. shovàrdesh
skin n. morthì, mooràv
skinned adj. mooravdò
skirt n. pogyà, foosta (s)
skirt-chaser n. loobehàri
sky n. del
slander n. drez

slander v. koodìnel
slap n. pàlma, cshamidinì
slaughter v. chinàv
slave n. robì, esiris
sled n. sànkya, sheynà
sledgehammer n. vàrya
sleep v. sootò, sov, sovàv
sleep n. sòìba
sleep over v. presovàv, sovlyaràv
sleep! imp. sov!
sleepy adj. sovavnò
sleeve n. bay
slim adj. sanò
slime n. tlàkos
Sliven Gypsies n. kutkàres
slow adv. polokès, poharì
slowing down n. màiba
slowly adv. pharès
small adj. tsiknò, zikarui, zikarlòo, harnòs
small finger n. tsikooroo angooshtoo
smaller adj. tsiknedèr
smell n. soong
smell of burning n. tsiknyà
smell v. soongàv
smile v. asàv
smoke n. thoov
smoke v. chadinàv
snake adj. sapanò

snake n. f. sapnì
snake n. m. sap
sneak v. chikyàv
snooze n. lìndra
snot n. lim
snotty adj. limalo
snout n. zoorlà
snow n. iv, yoov
snowdrop n. kookoochìn
snowy adj. ivalò
snub-nosed adj. hipalò
so achukà, **just so** gadavàsi
soap n. saòoni
sober adj. nernò
soberness n. nernipè
Sofia p.n. Barì dis (rare)
Sofia Moslem Gypsies n. arlìye
soft [sound wise] adj. tìhoo
soft [tactilely] adj. parus, kovlò
soft inside adj. andèr
sold adj. bikendò
soldier n. askèri, saldàtsi
some vàresavo
somebody else's adj. domanò
someone pron. dèkhoy, dek
something n. chìpa, cshìpota, vàreso
sometimes adv. dekhàna
somewhere adv. èkhate

son n. chavò, cshavò
son-in-law n. zhamootrò, gyoovèdis
song n. gilì
soon adv. birdèn
sorrel (bot.) n. shootlyahà
soul n. ozì , vogi,
soup n. zoomì, chorbà
sour adj. hoynalòo, shootlòo, shootlò
sow n. balì, baychì, balicshinì
sow v. suyzava (s)
spark n. svitka
sparrow n. chiriklò
speak v. horatìnav
spectacles n. gyozlikyà
speech n. chib
speed n. sig
speed v. makhàv
spend the night! imp. raktèr!
spend the night v. ratkeràv
sperm n. chàraybe (sl)
sphere n. kovlò
spicy adj. tharoo
spill v. cshorcheràva
spilled adj. cshordò
spinach n. spanakoos
spindel-makers n. lìngoorya
spindle n. katlì n.
spinning wheel n. chakrùk

spirit n. dèvi
spit n. cshoongàd, chigarà, shish
spit v. choongaràv, cshoongàdav
spittle n. hùrkolas
spleen n. dalakoos
split v. paravàv v.
spoon v. loy, rloy, roì
spout n. choochoori
sprain v. bertinàv
sprained adj. bertimè
sprain n. betrimè
spread out v. oostelizava
spread out! imp. postelizi!
spread v. boohlyaràv
spread [paint, etc.] v. makhàv
spring adj. kaynakì , honikàkeri, hanikàkeri
spring n. kaynàtsi
square n. megdùy
squashed adj. plakomè, kashkimè
steam ship n. parahòdoos
strike! imp. chalà!
St. George Day n. Edrelès
stab v. mooshkìzava
stables n. ahùri
stack-yard n. harmani
staff n. kilò
stall n. sergìya
stallion n. khoorò

stand n. sergìya
stand v. tèrgyovav
standing adj. ooshtinò
standing adv. terdindòs
star n. cherhèn
stare v. zepìzava
starry adj. cherhenyalò
stars n. pl. chulhuya
start on my way v. tsìdav
start v. astaràv
start moving v. lyàva
startle v. sepnìnav
startling adj. sèpniba
starvation n. bokhalipè
state adj. themootnò
state n. them
stay v. beshàv, teryava
stay behind v. acshàv
steal through v. chikyàv
steal v. cshoràva, choràva, tarashtù, choràv
stealing v. tarashtù
steel n. aptìn, absìn
steep adj. strùmno
step n. shtapka
step v. shtapkeràv, ooshtavàv
step! imp. ooshtàv! astapkèr!
steps [of a staircase] n. pl. basamàtsya
stick n. rooy, ruy

stiff adj. astardò
still adj. pàle
stink n. khan
stink v. kandàv
stirrup n. zenginì, zen
stocking n. zhoràpe
stolen adj. chordanò
stomach n. porl, hòola
stone n. bar, barl
stone/brick fence n. doovàri
stone/brick wall n. doovàri
stoning n. lamà
stony adj. barèstar
stop v. zaprìzava, acshàv
stop! imp. acsh! zàprezi!
store n. dyoogèi, dyookyàni
storm n. vrehòolka, balvàl
story n. paramisi
stove n. bof, bov (arm)
strain n. mètsiba, hents
strain v. metsìnav
stranger n. goorbeti
strangers n. straine (srb)
strangle v. tasavàv
strangled adj. tasavdò
straw adj. phoosano, phoos
strawberry n. hamtsùrus
street n. òolitsa, sokàtsi

strength n. zor
stress n. hents
stretch oneself v. gingyovav
stretch v. poravàv, boohlyaràv
stretched adj. boohlò
strike n. chala bè, chàliba, chàlaiba
strike v. lamàva (sl)
strike! imp. chalàv!
strike the aim v. chalavàv
string [of a musical instrument] n. tetivà
string n. dorì, kanàpi
string up n. nakhavàv
string! imp. nakhàv!
strong adj. zoralòo, hazlùs, zoralèste
strudel leaf n. pètoora
stubborness n. inàtsi, menyalipè
study n. sìkliba
study v. siklyovàv
study v. sikyàva
stuff up v. tuktìnav
stuffing n. ìchi
stump [of a vine] n. kyootitsi
stump n. moolookli
stunt n. bengipè
subsist v. nakhyaràv
such asavkà, asikà
such adj. kisavko
suck v. choochì piel

suckling lamb n. sookàlchitoos
suckling mother n. choochvalì
suckling n. choochyàte
suddenly adv. birdèn
suitcase n. mohtò
sulfur n. simpoori
summer n. lilày, nilài
sun n. khom, kham
Sunday n. kurkì, koorkò
sunrise n. drosìn, oopràlyavinate
superviser n. korkorbashì
supplied adj. resavdò
supply v. resavàv
support n. phikò
survive v. nakhyaràv
suspicion n. telalyakhà
swear v. sovlyadav, havsovèl
swear! imp. ha sovèl!
sweep v. shoolavàv
sweep! imp. shoolàv!
sweet adj. goodlò
sweeten v. gooderàva, goodlyaràv
sweetened adj. goodlyardò adj.
sweetness n. goodlipè
swell v. shoovlyovàv, kabardinàv
swept off adj. shoolavdò
swim v. plivinàv
swine n. balò, balì

swing n. kòona
swing v. kooninàv
swinging kòoniba
swollen adj. shoovlilò
sword n. harlò, harò
synagogue n. harvasàra

T
tablecloth n. oocsharibè
tail n.orì, por
tailored adj. sivdò
take an oath v. hav sovèl
take a breath v. tilya mozì
take down v. oohlyavàv
take out v. ikalàv
take v. lyàva, lav
take! imp. le!
taken adj. lendò
tale n. razprèyzila
talk in one's sleep v. bùlnoozyava
talk n. peryas-kerava, hòratiba
talkative adj. cshibalò
tall adj. oochò
tallow n. mom (pers)
tassel n. piskyòoy
taste v. tatìnav
taste! imp. tàtin!
tasteless adj. bilastsimi

tasty adj. bootlàchoo
tax n. dànakoos
teach v. sikavàv
teacher n. sikavnò
tear n. asvìn, àsva, àsoos
tear v. cshinàv
tearful adj. rovavnò
teaser n. azdrahìli
tell fortunes v. drabkeràv
ten n. desh
ten thousand n. desh milyà
tenant n. kirajìs
tenseness n. tetìki
tent n. katòoni, palàtka
tenth adj. dèshto
tepee [Gypsy camp style] n. kolìba
testicle n. tashaki
that is why adalkèske
that much adekhì, aboorkà, zòmka, asùmka,
    gadibòr
the art. f. i [the woman "i romnì"]
the art. m. o [the man "o rom"]
the back one adj. paloonò
the day after totasìya, tòtasya
the day before ich i rat
the end one adj. agorinò
theater n. teatroos
theft n. choribì, choribè

their pron. lìngoo
them pron. lin
then adv. zamàn
there adv. otkà, ohtè
there isn't nanày
they pron. odalà, odanà, yov
thicken v. thoolyovàv
thickness n. thoolipè
thief n. chor
thigh n. poorloo, chang
thin adj. kidhlò, sanò
thin out v. sanyovàv
things n. pl. nikamàva
think v. godisaràv
thinness n. sanopè
thirst n. troosh
thirsty adj. trooshalò
thirteen n. deshootrìn
thirty n. triànda
thirty thousand n. triyànda milyà
this kavkà
this adavkhà
this f. akaykà
this m. akavkà
this one adavkhà
this way adv. nakàriga
thistle n. haranoo korloo
thorn n. karò

thought n. dyooshyoondinè
thread n. thav, thov, dorì
thread v. nakhavàv
three n. trin
three hundred n. trìbshel
threshold n. pràgoos
throat n. korlò
throw on the ground v. dyàslis iphoo
    [lit. "gave him the ground"—
    wrestler's term]
throw v. cshivàv
throw! imp. cshiv!
throwing n. cshìiva
thrown adj. cshivtò
thrown away n. chikyàs
throw up v. ashàshibe
thumb n. baròo angooshtoo
thunder n. sèviba
thunder v. gurminèl
Thursday n. chetvùrtakoos, pevtsi
tick n. kurleshòos
tie v. pandàv
tiger n. tìguri
tile n. kirmìda n.
till ji [ji ahte "up to here"]
time n. vakùti, vakùtsi, tsìros, far, var (vlh)
tin-plate v. anolàv
tin-plating n. ànolima

tiny adj. hoordò
tip n. bakshìshi
tip of the knife n. nak
tired adj. kinilò
tiredness n. khìniba
tit n. choochì
to te
tobacco n. thoov
today adv. avdiès
today's adj. avdisootno
toe n. stoopì, angoosh
together adv. yekìsti, ekàek, ekhvariphàste
toilet n. kenèfi, zàhodoos
tombstone n. morìsko bar
tomcat n. tsitsanò
tomorrow adv. tasyà, tasià
tomorrow night adv. tasyà ki rat
tongs n. silyàva
tongue n. cshib, chip, chib
tonight adv. belyàke
tooth n. dand , dant
toothless adj. bi-dandàngoro
top n. hip
torn adj. ohtyazi, paravdò, paradoo
touchstone n. tochiloos
touch v. astaràv
touched in the head v. chavaldò
tough adj. zoralò

towards adv. ka
towel n. màrhama
town n. dis
track n. putèka
tradition n. chachipe (srb)
train n. tren
trained adj. siklò
transport v. nakhavàv
traveler n. dromootnò, droomalò
tread n. ooshtàv
treasure n. mangìn
treat n. cherpi
treat v. cherpìzava
treat! imp. cherpizi!
trench n. har
tress n. chochopi, kichooroos
tribe n. indais
trick n. bengipè
trip v. supninàv
tripped adj. supnimè
trivet n. piroostsì
trot n. rahvàni
trouble n. toonyà
trough for kneeding n. skavzì
trousers n. pantolyà
truck n. kamiònoos
trunk n. sandùtsi, mohtò
truth n. chachès

tub n. balùy
tube n. trubà
tuberculosis n. òftika
Tuesday n. vtòrnikoos
tulip n. lale
tumble v. valyànav
tumbled adj. valyamè
Turk n. horahày, horahùy
Turkey n. Horahanipè
turkey n. misìrka
Turkish adj. horahanò
Turkish coffee pot n. zhèzhbya
Turkish music n. manès
Turkish style adj. horahanes
Turkish woman n. horahnì
turn around v. ìrin
turn blue v. siynì
turn up v. boonzharàv [boonzharav me baya
    "turn up my sleeves"]
turn v. irìzava, bangyaràv
turn around v. irinàv
turned over adj. irimè
turnip n. ràdika
twelve n. dooshoodòoy
twentieth adj. bishtò
twenty n. besh, bish
twenty thousand n. bish milyà
twice adv. dòovar

twigs for basket weaving choochoonya, rayà
twigs n. pl. hoohoojà
twist v. izvìzava
two n. dooy
two hundred n. dòoyshel
two o'clock n. sahati dui
two thousand n. dooy milyà

U
ugly adj. gròzno
umbrella n. chadùri
uncle [on the father's brother] n. kàkoos
uncle [on the mother's side] n. dayjos
uncle n. kak
unclean adj. marime (srb)
under adv. deshemès
under part n. teloonipè
underneath adv. telàl
underpants n. sostèn
understand v. ahàyava
understanding adj. boojandò
understood v. ahaylè
undress v. nangyovàv
undressed adj. nangyardò
unexpectedly adv. nadjardò
unshaved adj. cshoralò
untidy adj. harabàti
untie v. pooteràv

up prep. ooprè, oprè, oprù
up to prep. ji
upon prep. e
upper adj. ooproonò
upside down adj. dèviri
upwards adv. naprù, noprù
urinate! imp. mootèr!
urine n. mootèr
us pron. amìn

V
vagina n. minch, mìnja
valley n. har
vampire n. chohanò
veel n. mooskarièskoro
vegetable garden n. bahchà
veil n. doovàki
village n. gav, gov
village adj. gavootnò
villager n. gavestàr
vine n. vitsa
vinegar n. shoot
vineyard n. rus, rez, ruz
violet n. kokòrchitoos, temenòoga
violin n. kemanès, dìvi, yòla
violin string wax n. ritsìna
visit n. misaferlìk
visitation n. dìkhiba

vixen n. lisìtsa
voice n. sèsi
vomit n. cshàdibe
vomit v. chadàv, cshadàv
vomit! imp. cshad!
vow n. sovèl

W
wage n. gyoonyòotsi
wager n. bas
wages n. zaplatà
wagon n. talìga
waist n. mashkàr
wait v. jaràv, zharàv
wait! imp. jar!
waiting n. jàriba
wake up v. jangavàv
wake up! imp. jàngalyov!
walk away v. dooryaràv man
walk n. phirdòo
walk v. phiràv, phiràva
walking adj. phirindòs
walking adv. pesh
walking n. phìriba
wall [of a room] n. doovàri
wall [of a yard] n. stràha
wall to wall wardrobe yooklòotsi
wallet n. kisì

walnut n. akhoòr
walnut tree n. akhurchìn
want v. mangàva, mangàv
war n. maribè
warm adj. tatò, tatòo
warm myself v. takyovàv
warm up v. takyaràv, tatyovàv
warmth n. tatipè
wash v. thovava, tovàv, tavàva, isthovàv
wash n. ìsthoiba
washtub n. balanì, gerdèy
washed adj. isthovdò
watch v. dandinàv, dendìnav
water adj. panyalò
water n. panì, puy
watermelon n. hurboozoo
water-mill n. dolàpi, asvày
waves n. dalgadès
wax n. mom
we pron. amè, amìn, amì
weak adj. kishlò
weakly adv. slàbo
wealth n. barvalipè, mangìn, barvaypì
wealthy adj. barvalò
weapon n. harlò
weariness n. khiniba
weather n. tsìroos
weave v. katàv, koovilà

wedding n. bayàv, byav
Wednesday n. tetràzi
weed n. bòoryanoos
week n. koorkò, koorkòo
weight n. tsìdiba, pharipè
welcome v. resàv
welcome! imp. res!
welcomed adj. restò
weld n. vràsi
weld v. vràsi dav
well adv. mishtò
well [water] adj. hanikàkeri
well n. boonàri, hanìk
well-risen [dough] adj. ooshlò
wet adj. soslò, sooslyardò
wet v. sooslyaràv
what int. savè, so, asvò, savì
what is the matter? int. sosì
what is your name? int. sar si to alav?
wheat n. jov, giv, zhìto
wheel n. kololàs, kololòos
when kàna
whence? dekathàr
where kàte
where from? kàtendar
where to? kàrik
where to? nakarìk?
whip n. bìchos

whirlpool n. vurtsi mi puy
whistle n. dooroolì
whistle v. shòldav
white adj. parnòo, parnò
white magic n. bahtali (srb)
whittle v. csholàv
who ko
who pron. kokà
whole sastò
whose f. kàskeri
whose m. kàskoro
wicked adj. joongalò
wickedness n. khanilipè
wicker-basket n. sùvi
wide adj. boohlò
widened adj. boohlyardò
widower n. phivlò
width n. boohlipè
wife n. romni
will ka [I will do it "ka kerav"]
will [future tense particle] ka
willow n. vùrba
win v. navìzava
wind n. balvàl
window n. penjerà, zhèmi
wine n. mol
wine bag n. myàhoos
wine merchant n. molyàri

wine producer n. molyàri

wing n. pak, phakh

wink n. dookalo

wink v. yakhalì cshiyav, yakhalòo cshelà [lit. "cast an eye"]

winnow v. oocshànav

winnowed adj. oocshdò

winnowing n. òochshaniba n.

winter adj. evendèskoro

winter n. evènd

wipe v. khosàva, khosàv

wipe! imp. khos!

wiped adj. khoslò

wise adj. gogyavèr, godiàsa, gozevèr

wise man adj. godiavèr manush, gozyavoo manoosh

wisely adv. gozyàsa adv.

wish n. bezèti

witch n. magyàrka

without hair adj. zar

wo! whoa! intj. khur!

wolf adj. roovanò

wolf n. roov

woman in child-birth n. lèhooso

woman n. roomi, joovli

womanizer n. changàkoo

woman's breast n. choochì

womb n. pelr, per

wood n. kash
woodcarver n. kopanàri
woodchopper n. veshtohàri, veshtìska rom
wooden adj. kashtoonò
wool n. poshom
word n. hortìna, alàv, hòrata
work n. bootì
work squad soldier n. troodovàtsi
work v. booti keràv
worker n. bookyarnò
worker's adj. bookyàrnegeri
world n. doonyàs, del
worm n. tsirmoo, kèrmo
wormy adj. kermalò
worn out adj. pooranò
wound n. pooknì
wounded adj. chalavdò
wrèstle! imp. ashàr!
wrapped adj. pakyardò
wrapper n. fàskya
wrestle v. asharàv, asharàva
wrestler n. asharnò, ashamò, pehlivùy
wrestling match n. àshariba
wrestling n. asharibè
wretched adj. gerò
wrinkle n. brùchka
wrinkled adj. kashkimè
write v. chinàva

Y

yard n. avlìn

yarn n. katlò

yawn v. hamsinàv, hastyàv

year n. bresh

yeast n. humer

yellow adj. zhultòo

yes va

yesterday adv. ich

yesterday's adj. ijootnò

yogurt drink n. erèy, arùy

yogurt n. gòorti

yoke n. bandrooki

You dad! voc. dàde!

You dear! voc. dàle!

You God! voc. Devlà!

You mom! voc. dàe!

You mother! voc. manè!

You Mother-in-law! voc. sasooè!

you pl. tooman

you pron. pl. toomìn

you pron. sing. toot

you sing. too

You uncle! voc. dayjo!

young adj. ternòo, ternò

young looking adj. ternyòl

your pron. pl. toomaròo, toomarò

your pron. sing. toròo, torlòo
yours pron. terò, terì
youth n. ternipè
youthful adj. ternèngoro

The Hippocrene Mastering Series

These imaginative courses, designed for both individual and classroom use, assume no previous knowledge of the language. The unique combination of practical exercises and step-by-step grammar emphasizes a functional approach to new scripts and their vocabularies. Everyday situations and local customs are explored variously through dialogues, newspaper extracts, drawings and photos. Cassettes are available for each language.

MASTERING FRENCH
288 pages • 5½ x 8½ • 0-87052-055-5 • $14.95pb • (511)
2 Cassettes: • 0-87052-060-1 USA • $12.95 • (512)
MASTERING ADVANCED FRENCH
348 pages • 5½ x 8½ • 0-7818-0312-8 • W • $14.95pb • (41)
2 Cassettes: • 0-7818-0313-6 • W • $12.95 • (54)
MASTERING GERMAN
340 pages • 5½ x 8½ • 0-87052-056-3 • $11.95pb • (514)
2 Cassettes: • 0-87052-061-X USA • $12.95 • (515)
MASTERING ITALIAN
360 pages • 5½ x 8½ • 0-87052-057-1 • USA • $11.95pb • (517)
2 Cassettes: 0-87052-066-0 • USA • $12.95 • (521)
MASTERING ADVANCED ITALIAN
278 pages • 5½ x 8½ • 0-7818-0333-0 • W • $14.95pb • (160)
2 Cassettes: 0-7818-0334-9 • W • $12.95 • (161)
MASTERING JAPANESE
368 pages • 5½ x 8½ • 0-87052-923-4 • USA • $14.95pb
• (523)
2 Cassettes: • 0-87052-983-8 (USA • $12.95 • (524)
MASTERING NORWEGIAN
183 pages • 5½ x 8½ • 0-7818-0320-9 • W • $14.95pb • (472)
MASTERING POLISH
288 pages • 5½ x 8½ • 0-7818-0015-3 • W • $14.95pb • (381)
2 Cassettes: • 0-7818-0016-1 • W • $12.95 • (389)

MASTERING RUSSIAN
278 pages • 5½ x 8½ • 0-7818-0270-9 • W • $14.95pb • (11)
2 Cassettes: • 0-7818-0271-7 • W • $12.95 • (13)
MASTERING SPANISH
338 pages • 5½ x 8½ • 0-87052-059-8 USA • $11.95 • (527)
2 Cassettes: • 0-87052-067-9 USA • $12.95 • (528)
MASTERING ADVANCED SPANISH
326 pages • 5½ x 8½ • 0-7818-0081-1 • W • $14.95pb • (413)
2 Cassettes: • 0-7818-0089-7 • W • $12.95 • (426)

Hippocrene's Beginner's Series

Do you know what it takes to make a phone call in Russia? Or how to get through customs in Japan? This new language instruction series shows how to handle oneself in typical situations by introducing the business person or traveler not only to the vocabulary, grammar, and phrases of a new language, but also the history, customs, and daily practices of a foreign country.

The Beginner's Series consists of basic language instruction, which also includes vocabulary, grammar, and common phrases and review questions, along with cultural insights, interesting historical background, the country's basic facts and hints about everyday living-driving, shopping, eating out, and more.

BEGINNER'S ASSYRIAN
185 pages • 5 x 9 • 0-7818-0677-1 • $11.95pb • (763)
BEGINNER'S CHINESE
150 pages • 5½ x 8 • 0-7818-0566-x • $14.95pb • (690)
BEGINNER'S BULGARIAN
207 pages • 5½ x 8½ • 0-7818-0300-4 • $9.95pb • (76)
BEGINNER'S CZECH
200 pages • 5½ x 8½ • 0-7818-0231-8 • $9.95pb • (74)
BEGINNER'S ESPERANTO
400 pages • 5½ x 8½ • 0-7818-0230-x • $14.95pb • (51)

BEGINNER'S HUNGARIAN
200 pages • 5½ x 7 • 0-7818-0209-1 • $7.95pb • (68)
BEGINNER'S JAPANESE
200 pages • 5½ x 8½ • 0-7818-0234-2 • $11.95pb • (53)
BEGINNER'S LITHUANIAN
230 pages • 6 x 9 • 0-7818-0678-X • $19.95pb • (764)
BEGINNER'S MAORI
121 pages • 5½ x 8½ • 0-7818-0605-4 • $8.95pb • (703)
BEGINNER'S PERSIAN
150 pages • 5½ x 8 • 0-7818-0567-8 • $14.95pb • (696)
BEGINNER'S POLISH
200 pages • 5½ x 8½ • 0-7818-0299-7 • $9.95pb • (82)
BEGINNER'S ROMANIAN
200 pages • 5½ x 8½ • 0-7818-0208-3 • $7.95pb • (79)
BEGINNER'S RUSSIAN
200 pages • 5½ x 8½ • 0-7818-0232-6 • $9.95pb • (61)
BEGINNER'S SICILIAN
158 pages • 5½ x 8½ • 0-7818-0640-2 • $11.95pb • (7 16)
BEGINNER'S SWAHILI
200 pages • 5½ x 8½ • 0-7818-0335-7 • $9.95pb • (52)
BEGINNER'S UKRAINIAN
130 pages • 5½ x 8½ • 0-7818-0443-4 • $11.95pb • (88)
BEGINNER'S VIETNAMESE
517 pages • 7 x 10 • 30 lessons • 0-7818-0411-6 • $19.95pb
• (253)
BEGINNER'S WELSH
210 pages • 5½ x 8½ • 0-7818-0589-9 • $9.95pb • (712)

The Dictionary & Phrasebook Series

AUSTRALIAN DICTIONARY AND PHRASEBOOK
131 pages • 3¾ x 7 • 1,500 entries • 0-7818-0539-2 • W
• $11.95pb • (626)

**BASQUE-ENGLISH/ ENGLISH-BASQUE
DICTIONARY AND PHRASEBOOK**
240 pages • 3¾ x 7 • 1,500 entries • 0-7818-0622-4 • W
• $11.95pb • (751)

**BOSNIAN-ENGLISH/ENGLISH-BOSNIAN
DICTIONARY AND PHRASEBOOK**
175 pages • 3¾ x 7 • 1,500 entries • 0-7818-0596-1 • W
• $11.95pb • (691)

**BRETON-ENGLISH/ENGLISH-BRETON
DICTIONARY AND PHRASEBOOK**
131 pages • 3¾ x 7 • 1,500 entries • 0-7818-0540-6 • W
• $11.95pb • (627)

**BRITISH-AMERICAN/AMERICAN-BRITISH
DICTIONARY AND PHRASEBOOK**
160 pages • 3¾ x 7 • 1,400 entries • 0-7818-0450-7 • W
• $11.95pb • (247)

**CHECHEN-ENGLISH/ENGLISH-CHECHEN
DICTIONARY AND PHRASEBOOK**
160 pages • 3¾ x 7 • 1,400 entries • 0-7818-0446-9 • NA
• $11.95pb • (183)

**GEORGIAN-ENGLISH/ENGLISH-GEORGIAN
DICTIONARY AND PHRASEBOOK**
150 pages • 3¾ x 7 • 1,300 entries • 0-7818-0542-2 • W
• $11.95pb • (630)

**EASTERN ARABIC-ENGLISH/ENGLISH-EASTERN
ARABIC DICTIONARY AND PHRASEBOOK**
142 pages • 3¾ x 7 • 2,200 entries • 0-7818-0685-2 • W
• $11.95pb • (774)

ILOCANO-ENGLISH/ENGLISH-ILOCANO DICTIONARY AND PHRASEBOOK
174 pages • 5 x 8 • 0-7818-0642-9 • $11.95pb • (718)

IRISH-ENGLISH/ENGLISH-IRISH DICTIONARY AND PHRASEBOOK
160 pages • 3¾ x 7 • 1,400 entries/phrases • 0-87052-110-1 • NA • $7.95pb • (385)

LINGALA-ENGLISH/ENGLISH-LINGALA DICTIONARY AND PHRASEBOOK
120 pages • 3¾ x 7 • 0-7818-0456-6 • W • $11.95pb • (296)

MALTESE-ENGLISH/ENGLISH-MALTESE DICTIONARY AND PHRASEBOOK
175 pages • 3¾ x 7 • 1,500 entries • 0-7818-0565-1 • W • $11.95pb • (697)

POLISH DICTIONARY AND PHRASEBOOK
252 page • 5½ x 8½ • 0-7818-0134-6 • W • $11.95pb • (192)

RUSSIAN DICTIONARY AND PHRASEBOOK, Revised
256 pages • 5½ x 8½ • 3,000 entries • 0-7818-0190-7 • W • $9.95pb • (597)

SLOVAK-ENGLISH/ENGLISH-SLOVAK DICTIONARY AND PHRASEBOOK
180 pages • 3¾ x 7 • 1,300 entries • 0-7818-0663-1 • W • $13.95pb • (754)

UKRAINIAN DICTIONARY AND PHRASEBOOK
205 pages • 5½ x 8½ • 3,000 entries • 0-7818-0188-5 • $11.95pb • (28)

All prices are subject to change without prior notice. To order Hippocrene Books, contact your local bookstore, call (718) 454-2366, or write to: Hippocrene Books, 171 Madison Ave. New York, NY 10016. Please enclose check or money order adding $5.00 shipping (UPS) for the first book and $.50 for each additional title.